Story Starters for Group Times

Story Starters for Group Times

Ann S. Epstein, PhD

HIGHSCOPE
PRESS®

Ypsilanti, Michigan

Published by
HighScope® Press
A division of the
HighScope Educational Research Foundation
600 North River Street
Ypsilanti, Michigan 48198-2898
734.485.2000, Fax: 734.485.0704
Orders: 800.40.PRESS; Fax: 800.442.4FAX; highscope.org
E-mail: *press@highscope.org*

Editor: Joanne Tangorra, *HighScope Press Editor*
Design and Production: Judy Seling, Seling Design
Cover Illustration: Judy Seling, Seling Design
Photography:
Bob Foran — 33, 169
Gregory Fox — 5, 11, 13, 34, 171
HighScope Staff — All other photos

Library of Congress Cataloging-in-Publication Data
Epstein, Ann S.
  Story starters for group times / Ann S. Epstein.
      p. cm.
  Includes bibliographical references.
  ISBN 978-1-57379-474-9 (soft cover : alk. paper) 1. Storytelling. 2. Language arts (Early childhood) 3. Group work in education. I. Title.
  LB1042.E67 2010
  372.67'7—dc22
                                        2010003994

Printed in the United States of America
10 9 8 7 6 5 4 3 2 1

Contents

Acknowledgements

Writing *Story Starters for Group Times* was a happy convergence of two of my main interests. Professionally, I have been writing about early childhood for many decades. This book not only reflects my belief that we learn best from the narratives we hear and tell throughout our lives, but also that education must provide young children with stories in every domain of their development. Stories are not only about language and literacy, they also enliven the worlds of mathematics, science, physical development, and the arts. Personally, I also write and publish short fiction and creative nonfiction. I use what I have learned about human nature — from children and the adults who care for them — to spur the flights of fancy and characters that inhabit my stories.

This book could not have been written without inspiration from all of these sources. I am eternally grateful to my colleagues in the Early Childhood Division at HighScope for their ongoing support and encouragement. In particular, I want to thank Sue Gainsley and Shannon Lockhart for reviewing the manuscript and giving me detailed feedback based on their many years of telling stories to and conducting group times with preschool children. They provided valuable insight into how the stories could be used as the starting point — not an end in themselves — to get children involved using materials and discovering ideas in their own creative ways.

I also want to thank my editor Joanne Tangorra for asking the questions that made the writing clearer for those who will read and use this book. When writers are immersed in projects we love, a pair of outside eyes can help us see that what appears crystal clear to us may be downright misty to others. As you read this book and find yourself thinking, "I get it!" you can join me in thanking Joanne for bringing clarity to the manuscript.

The contributions of other members of the production team were also vital in making this book a reality. Katie Bruckner typed each successive revision of the manuscript so everyone involved was looking at the same story on the same page as we moved to finalize the book. The sprightly cover and straightforward layout are thanks to Judy Seling, who has designed so many of the other books in HighScope's Teacher Idea series.

I am also indebted to the members of my creative writing group. In the ten years we've been meeting, I have never left a workshop without having learned something new about the art and craft of writing. Finally, I want to thank the young children whose imaginations and love of learning energize all of us to invent stories every day.

Stories are made up of characters, the settings in which they act and think, and the events that transpire. In *Story Starters for Group Times,* teachers and children are the characters, the early childhood classroom is the setting, and the story is the first event in the group time that unfolds. Let the children write the rest of the story.

— A. S. Epstein

PART ONE: INTRODUCTION TO STORY STARTERS

1

Introduction to Story Starters

A preschool teacher began a mathematics small-group time called "Bears on a Boat" with the following story: *Once upon a time a family of bears wanted to go on a boat ride.* She put a small block in the middle of the table and 10 counting bears next to it. *"I think we should all go," said one bear. "There's not enough room for everyone," said another. "Oh dear, how will we figure out how many can go?" said a third.* The teacher put five bears on the block (they took up most but not all the space), distributed a block and set of bears to each child, and said, *Can you help the bears solve their problem?* Midway through the activity, she set out story props the children

Used as a lead-in to small- and large-group activities, story starters enhance children's learning in virtually every curriculum content area — mathematics (above), language and literacy, science, physical development, and the creative arts.

could use if they chose, such as blue paper and fabric pieces for "water," washcloths they could shake to make "waves," and trays for "rafts."

Children used the materials in different ways. Some tried to squeeze all the bears on the block, others put them on and knocked them off. Several children counted (not always correctly) and a couple "added" and "subtracted" bears in different combinations. They talked about the boat being *too full, all empty,* and needing to be *longer so all the bears could go for a ride at the same time.* A few children lined up their boats together so more bears could fit on. As they worked, children added their own ideas to the story:

— *This first bear is the captain.*

— *Two fell off and alligators ate them. Now there's only 1-2-3 bears left.*

— *There's gonna be a storm. They better all go back!*

— *What if a gazillion more bears came to the lake?*

— *First the blue bears went for a ride, then the red ones.*

— *The bears that didn't fit went swimming instead.*

— *No, they went for a ride on the train!*

In the above vignette, the teacher used a **story starter** to encourage children to explore ideas about number (counting; all, some, none; more, fewer) and geometry (full, empty; fit). A story starter is a short narrative for introducing children to the content of a small- or large-group activity. Its purpose is to get them involved in working with the materials and thinking about the concepts that are the primary focus of that activity. It also opens the door to unanticipated discoveries about materials, characters, events, and big (gazillion-size) ideas!

These short stories naturally enhance young children's language and literacy skills. Children listen to and try to comprehend the narrative, describe their actions and observations as they work with materials, and add their own imaginative details. Stories can also be the starting point to enhance learning in virtually every other content area — mathematics, science, physical development, and the creative arts (art, pretend play, and music).

The Development of Storytelling in Young Children

Storytelling with young children is a collaborative and interactive process. Children rarely listen passively to an engaging story told by an adult. They make comments (e.g., *I bet that building was as tall as a mountain*), ask questions (e.g., *Did it hurt when he fell down?*), and contribute their own narrative ideas (e.g., *Then he gobbled up another one!*). Likewise, when children tell stories, they incorporate ideas from one another, as in the following example:

> First child: *The baby is sick.*
>
> Second child: *It has a fever.*
>
> First child: *It's a really high fever. The baby has to go to the hospital!*

Children are also inspired by comments from interested adults:

> Child: *She has to cross the river to save the kitty.*
>
> Adult: *I wonder how she'll cross the river.*
>
> Child: *She's riding on the back of an alligator!*

A child's ability to be an active participant in this storytelling process grows along with his or her cognitive and linguistic development.

According to professor and researcher Stephanie Curenton (2006), children start to tell stories around age two, beginning with simple, single-event narratives. Storytelling continues to develop throughout the preschool years, with a coherent plot structure emerging around age five. By the time they enter school, children have picked up the storytelling norms of their culture from repeated verbal exchanges with family members, early childhood teachers, religious leaders, and other members of their communities. In the elementary grades and into adolescence, children expand their narratives by adding details, elaborating themes, and evaluating characters and events (McCabe, 1997). Although young children's stories are brief and most often deal with a past event or simple fantasy, they "contain a wealth of information about what the children remember, what they are feeling, and how they resolve interpersonal and psychological conflicts" (Curenton, 2006, p. 80).

Developmental psychologists Greta Fein and Vivian Paley were pioneers in recognizing the importance of interactive storytelling — adults and children creating stories together — in early childhood. According to Goncu & Klein (2001), Fein not only observed how storytelling with young children promoted their literacy development, but also called attention to the social origins and significance of sharing stories with them. Professor and early childhood teacher Carrie Whaley comments that children do not just enjoy listening to stories, "they are natural storytellers themselves. They build story frameworks to help themselves understand the world and incorporate story scenarios into their play" (2002, p. 31).

Vivian Paley, a long-time teacher and teacher-educator at the University of Chicago's Laboratory School, also emphasized the central role of chil-

dren's storytelling and story acting in their play and learning. She said, "A day without storytelling is, for me, a disconnected day. I cannot remember what is real to the children without their stories to anchor fantasy and purpose" (Paley, 1990, p. 3).

Paley's teachings led early childhood specialist Sally Hurwitz to realize that "children don't look at a story the way adults do; rather, they see themselves playing inside a story. They

Young children learn the storytelling norms of their culture as the result of repeated exchanges with the people around them, including their family members and early childhood teachers.

invent the rules, roles, and circumstances that make the story their own. They try through story to resolve the issues that affect their lives. In storytelling, children try new vocabulary, extend their narrative skills, exercise control of their learning, and become models and learners. Storytelling guarantees success and enhances self-esteem" (Hurwitz, 2001, p. 90).

The Importance of Stories in Early Learning

When adults use stories to start a group-time activity, and encourage children to add their own narrative elements through the use of materials, actions, and language, all these possibilities for learning are presented to children. As they work with the materials and ideas, they personalize the story and convert its characters and events to their own purposes. For example, a small-group time focused on counting (one-to-one correspondence) might begin with the adult telling a story about finding enough bowls and spoons for an ice cream party. Children can "personalize" the story to explore basic counting principles, for example, by tallying the number of friends invited, counting out two different colors of bowls to make up the total (composing and decomposing the whole and its parts), and so on. As they choose elements of the starter story to tell and act out their own stories, children construct meaning and understanding.

An acute observer and relentless documenter, Paley also saw stories as a "connecting rod [that] bridges what children already know, what they want to know, and what they don't yet know" (Hurwitz, 2001, p. 89). *The Intentional Teacher,* by the author of this book, makes the same observation, "Children comprehend things by linking what they are learning to what they already know" (Epstein, 2007b, p. 31). When used as "starters" for group times, therefore, stories can help children make connections between materials and ideas, skills and concepts, observations and conclusions. A story helps children link what they know about a subject to new knowledge and skills. For example, for children who know color names, a story about an overturned basket of colored balls can open an activity on sorting, patterning, direction and speed of movement, and so on.

Just as the stories children hear can spark learning, children in turn can express learning through the stories they tell. Vygotsky says that "in play a child behaves beyond his average age, above his daily behavior; in play it is as though he were a head taller than himself" (1978, p. 102). In other words, children use play to advance their level of thinking and understanding. They test out ideas and relationships, and adjust their reasoning according to how their play "plays out." Early childhood professors Celia Genishi and Rebekah Fassler add that "child-watchers know that when children engage in pretend or dramatic play, they take on characteristics of people who behave and speak differently from themselves. Children can display what they are learning in novel ways" (1999, p. 71). The stories children take part in inventing help them give expression to their observations and emerging ideas, and often surprise us with their acuity and wisdom.

While much has been written about storytelling with young children in general, there are no publications specific to why and how to use story starters as a lead-in to learning. Certainly, these two story-based activities have characteristics and benefits in common, but there are fundamental differences when a story is used to

The stories children take part in inventing give expression to their thoughts, observations, and ideas.

launch another activity rather than serving as the focus of the activity itself, as in storytelling. For example, a story starter is shorter and simpler than a stand-alone story, so children can quickly turn their attention to the materials and ideas that are the focus of the activity. In a stand-alone story the narrative is typically resolved by the story's end. A story starter is more open-ended so children can use the materials and events to elaborate on their own ongoing tale; there's no need for an "ending" or resolution. (For more information on how stand-alone stories and story starters differ, see chapter 3.)

This book will give you the background to understand the similarities and differences between extended storytelling and using brief story starters to initiate group-time exploration and learning. You will learn why story starters can be an enjoyable and effec-tive lead-in to group times and how to use them with the children in your classroom. You will also find 84 story starters on a wide variety of topics, plus guidelines for creating your own story starters and using them to suc-cessfully promote early learning.

How This Book Is Organized

Part One (Chapters 1 to 4) of *Story Starters for Group Times* presents an overview of why and how to use story starters to begin small- and large-group times with young children. It describes the benefits of storytelling for early literacy development, application to other content areas, and relationship to promoting overall school readiness. General considerations for conduct-ing group times, with an emphasis on active participatory learning, are summarized, followed by strategies for using "story starters" in this context.

Part Two contains seven chapters, each covering one content area:

Chapter 5: Language, Literacy, and Communication

Chapter 6: Mathematics

Chapter 7: Science and Technology

Chapter 8: Art

Chapter 9: Pretend Play

Chapter 10: Music

Chapter 11: Physical Development and Health

At the beginning of each chapter is a brief list of the important learning that takes place in that content area during the preschool years. The chapter then presents 12 activities, each with the following information:

- Activity title — The title of the activity

- Content area — The primary content area that the activity focuses on

- Activity description — A statement of what children do and learn during the activity

- Time of day — Whether the activity is designed for small- or large-group time

- Materials — The materials needed to carry out the activity, specifying those for each child and teacher, materials to share, and back-up materials

- Story starter — The story used to begin the activity

- Scaffolding children's learning – Strategies to support and extend children's learning during the activity, including how to use *vocabulary words* (basic words as well as "rare" or infrequently used words) when conversing with children about their actions and ideas

- Follow-up ideas — Suggestions to extend the learning that occurs during the activity throughout the program day and in different areas of the classroom.

Part Three (Chapters 12 and 13) will help you create your own story starters and use them to carry out small- and large-group times in your program. It contains a checklist to help you generate ideas and use the principles of active learning and effective story starters. There is also an activity plan, like the one used to present the activities in this book, with guidelines to help you record your story starters and group-time implementation plans.

2

The Role of Stories and Storytelling in Early Literacy Development

In recent years, a great deal of emphasis has been placed on reading to young children and teaching them to read, for example, in the Early Reading First initiative of the U.S. Department of Education. While applauding this interest, researchers David Dickinson and Patton Tabors suggest caution, noting "Of particular concern is the possibility that early literacy efforts will take a single-minded focus on print-related dimensions and fail to recognize that *oral language* is the foundation of early literacy" (2002, p. 10).

Oral Language and Early Literacy Development

To support their claim, Dickinson and Tabors cite the results of a longitudinal study, begun in 1987, that followed low-income (Head Start-eligible) children from preschool to high school. Researchers found that the follow-

ing three factors were positively and significantly related to later literacy success:

- Exposure to *varied vocabulary*

- Opportunities to be part of conversations that use *extended discourse*

- Experiences in *home and classroom environments* that are cognitively and linguistically stimulating

Listening and speaking — oral language — are two essential ways that children take part in these foundational experiences. And stories and storytelling help to create these language-rich opportunities.

All three literacy factors identified in the longitudinal research reported by Dickinson & Tabors (2002) are prominent in storytelling, and can be intentionally enhanced to maximize young children's encounters with oral language. (For more on the importance of oral language in early literacy development, see sidebar below.)

Varied vocabulary. A great deal of vocabulary is acquired before children become literate. It is estimated that a child needs a vocabulary of 6,000 to 7,000 words to converse fluently, and 8,000 to 9,000 words to read and understand text (Jalongo, 2008). Stories are an enjoyable and effective way to expand children's vocabulary, letting them hear and practice familiar words while also exposing them to rare or less frequently used words.

Storytelling with preschoolers "introduces them to object, action, and idea words" (Hohmann & Adams, 2008, p. 25). In telling stories, adults can use the vocabulary-building strategies that research shows are especially important for young children, namely, incorporating familiar synonyms and simple definitions, helping children

Oral Language and Early Literacy

There is overwhelming evidence that early vocabulary development plays a positive and significant role in the later acquisition of reading ability (National Reading Panel, 2000; Neuman & Dickinson, 2001). The dramatic impact of this relationship emerged in the classic study by psychologists Betty Hart and Todd Risley (1999), which revealed differences favoring children from middle class over lower class families in the number and variety of words young children hear. This early language exposure was positively and significantly related to the subsequent size of their vocabularies, and to their literacy skills and overall academic success.

As a result of this research, the importance of oral language experiences for later literacy development is emphasized in position papers and guidelines for practice, such as the joint publication of the International Reading Association and National Association for the Education of Young Children (Neuman, Copple, & Bredekamp, 2000), as well as the program performance standards and child outcomes required by Head Start (U. S. Department of Health and Human Services, 2008) and many states and local school districts.

A prominent study reported in *Pediatrics* (Zimmerman, Gilkerson, Richards, Christakis, Xu, Gray, & Yapanel, 2009) found that "adult-child conversations are robustly associated with healthy language development" (p. 342) and concluded that adults should be encouraged to provide speech input to young children by "talking to them, reading them books, and telling them stories" (p. 347). Two-way conversations in which children talk as well as listen are particularly important in later language development. Moreover, during these conversations, it is valuable for children to not only hear basic vocabulary words, but also to hear "rare" or infrequent words (that is, words that adults do not typically use with children or that children are not likely to hear). A varied vocabulary, and more complex sentence structure, acquaints children with the rich world of language.

Story-based activities are an important part of oral language development, particularly vocabulary building.

draw inferences and make comparisons, referring to the child's prior experiences, and using the context of the story to convey what words mean (Gaffney, Ostrosky, & Hemmeter, 2008). It is easier for children to learn new and unusual words when they are associated with familiar ones in an engaging narrative.

Just as important as the vocabulary children hear is the number and variety of words they are encouraged to say themselves. Therefore, story-based activities in which children can use and talk about materials, act out ideas in words as well as gestures, and add to or elaborate on the story in their

own words, is an important part of oral language development in general, and vocabulary-building in particular. For example, in a small-group time pretend-play activity, children may pretend to cook a giant pot of "stew" for very hungry dinosaurs. The story starter can include the names of foods that are familiar (peas) and unfamiliar (lentils), as well as things that children from different backgrounds eat at home. The narrative can introduce nouns less frequently used with children, such as the words *ingredient* and *spice,* action words (verbs) such as *gurgle* and *grate,* and descriptive words (adjectives) such as *salty* and *bland.* When children hear these words in the context of the story, they will begin to use them independently as they make up tales to accompany their own "cooking."

Extended discourse. Listening to stories read or told by adults is not enough to help young children develop a base for later literacy. They must also engage in thought and dialogue to build comprehension and expressive language skills. As children "share" a story with adults, their narrative acquires coherence. Says professor and researcher Rebecca Isbell, "Active listening and co-creating with the teacher serve as catalysts for generating ideas at the intersection of the story and children's own experiences" (2002, p. 27). Adults scaffold children's ideas with prompts, such as *I wonder what will happen next?* or *Then what did they do (say)?* (p. 28).

Based on early literacy research, HighScope and many other early childhood curricula therefore emphasize that "language and literacy skills are best promoted when reading and storytelling are interactive" (Epstein, 2007a, p. 119). Children benefit from seeing, hearing, and participating when adults read aloud or tell them stories, that is, by making comments, and asking and answering questions. For the same reason, children enhance their expressive language vocabulary by reading and telling stories to adults and to one another.

[Note: Telling stories aloud is also different from reading stories printed on the page. See sidebar below for a comparison of story reading and storytelling.]

Researchers Mary Jane Moran and Jennifer Jarvis (2001) use the

The Difference Between Story Reading and Storytelling

Reading stories from books and telling stories both support language and literacy development, but they also differ in significant ways. Early childhood professor and researcher Rebecca Isbell (2002) notes that storytelling is often more personal. The *storyteller* focuses on the listener, while the *story reader* pays more attention to the text (or goes back and forth between listener and text). The language of storytelling is also more informal than printed text, just as spoken language is less formal than written language. While story reading and storytelling both depend on vocal expression, storytelling is more often accompanied by other cues such as body language. It is also more likely to involve materials — such as props, puppets, or dolls — which further enhance the richness of the experience for the listener. Storytelling promotes *expressive* language (the words a child actually says) while reading emphasizes *receptive* language (the words a child understands but may not yet say). Finally, storytelling helps and encourages children to generate their own stories, which in turn inspires their interest in dictation and later in writing on their own (Nelson, 1989).

term "co-narration" to describe the shared experience of adults and children creating stories together. Adults make comments and ask and answer questions; children offer observations about characters and events or suggest directions for the story to proceed. In addition to promoting language and literacy skills, co-narration cements the sense of community in the classroom. Shared stories enhance the level of detail in the narratives and encourage social interaction.

Extending dialogue through interactive storytelling can be applied to using story starters too. Gathered for small- or large-group time, children watch and listen to the adult's opening narrative, describe and interpret what they hear and observe, and contribute their suggestions. As they begin to work with their own set of materials, children often construct and elaborate stories to go along with their actions. Follow-up discussion further encourages them to express their ideas, solve problems with materials, and listen to the descriptions and narratives of others.

Storytelling can also evoke visual images, especially when accompanied by varied and interesting materials, which in turn leads to further descriptive dialogue. For example, a science small-group time designed to acquaint children with the use of magnifying

In co-narration, adults and children create stories together. These shared stories promote language and literacy skills as well as a sense of community in the classroom.

glasses can start with a story about a planet where even the tiniest parts of objects look very big. The narrative provides a starting point for children to describe what different materials look like when they see them with their naked eye compared to the more detailed view they see through a magnifying lens.

The conversations through which adults extend story ideas also help children go beyond the "here and now." While children mostly talk about the immediate setting or context, stories encourage them to engage in "nonimmediate" or "decontextualized" talk — talk that is not bound by the immediate situation or context. To understand printed text, children cannot depend on context or gestures, such as facial expressions. These cues are not on the page. Stories, like pretend play, help them imagine what is not physically present. When teachers introduce story starters as a jumping-off point for children's own actions and ideas, the ensuing dialogue prepares pre-readers to also imagine what is not immediately before them when they encounter the printed page. Language becomes a stand-in for actual people, objects, actions, and events.

To be most effective at group times, extended discourse should actively involve all the adult and child participants. If the rest of the children are just listening while an adult has a lengthy conversation with one child, they may "tune out." Techniques for including everyone include repeating ideas to the rest of the group and encouraging children to talk to and build on one another's contributions. Teachers can also rotate, engaging in extended discourse with one or two individuals while others work with materials, then moving to the next child who appears open to conversation. [Note: Interrupting a child's actions to have a conversation can cut short the child's activities. It is more effective to watch and listen, or silently imitate what the child is doing, and wait for the child to initiate the conversation. Then the adult can engage in extended discourse that follows the child's lead.]

For example, after leading in to an activity with a story, the adult can encourage children to imagine what would happen if events had transpired differently. One teacher used a physical development story starter about mice having a race to see who could *scamper* (a new word) through a line of tires in the shortest or fastest time. After the children tried different ways of jumping as fast as they could, the teacher said, *Suppose the mice wanted to see who could take the longest (slowest) time?* The children shared ideas for crawling over rims, going backwards, and circling the tire before moving to the next one. As they talked about their actions, they were not only moving their bodies in different ways, they were also using many words to explore concepts about space (a component of mathematics) and time (an aspect of science and technology), such as *over, under, inside, outside, around, across, forward, backward, fast,* and *slow.* In this way, activities in one content area often lead to exploration and enhanced understanding in other content areas.

Environments that support oral language. The advantages of reading books with children are thoroughly documented and widely publicized.

However, the contributions made by other environmental factors to language and literacy development should not be overlooked. Any setting that expands children's knowledge and skills — regardless of the subject matter — can enhance their oral language capabilities. Put another way, children who are actively engaged and interested in what they are doing will have something to talk about. Curiosity prompts them to ask questions (a more effective learning tool than being *asked* questions), discuss their actions and observations, and share their excitement of discovery and pride in accomplishment.

Dickinson and Tabors (2001) report that when teachers extend children's experiences (for example, providing role-play props after a field trip) and plan group activities with learning goals in mind, literacy development is enhanced. Stories are one way to engage young children in this learning process. A story starter can introduce them to new materials or new ways of using and thinking about familiar materials. It can set up situations that encourage children to pose and solve problems they have not considered before. Storytelling can emphasize phonological awareness through rhyme, alliteration, and repetition (*Fee, Fie, Fo, Fum* or *I'll huff and I'll puff and I'll blow your house down*). The fun of storytelling is contagious, especially when teller and listener switch roles. Story starters even offer a double benefit — the oral language

Story starters can introduce children to new materials — like these giant pine cones — or to new ways of thinking about and using familiar materials such as shells.

experience of the story plus the added value of the activity's content focus (mathematics, science, art, and so on).

For example, after an art museum field trip, one teacher told a story about children who made so much art, they decided to open their own museum. She provided building materials (blocks, shelves), writing tools (blank labels, markers), and artwork made by the children or contributed by their families. They used the story idea and materials to create their own museums, either individually or in small collaborative groups. Based on the field trip and vocabulary words added by the teacher, the children talked about *mounting* paintings on the wall, displaying *sculptures* on *pedestals,* and writing the artist, title and *medium* on the label. At work (choice) time, some children continued playing "art museum" by pretending to be tour leaders, guards, artists, and visitors.

Storytelling and School Readiness

School readiness is more than academic preparedness. It combines a range of cognitive and social skills that allows children to listen, comprehend, remember concepts, and maintain relationships. Storytelling can contribute to the young child's development in all these domains. According to one early childhood expert, "Oral storytelling is a tool that equally promotes and masterfully synchronizes children's cognitive and socioemotional development. In the cognitive domain, storytelling promotes children's language and literacy; in the social-emotional domain, storytelling promotes children's self-identity, social-emotional reasoning, and problem solving" (Curenton, 2006, p. 81).

Storytelling promotes **language and literacy.** Storytelling is *decontextualized talk,* talk not bound by people, objects, or events in the immediate environment (see "extended discourse" above). Whether children are relating real-life experiences or fantasies, their stories are about events that did or might happen, not something going on at that moment. Decontextualized talk develops higher-order thinking skills (see opposite page) such as memory and planning, and promotes comprehension. Research shows comprehension of oral stories is tied to general cognitive, language, and emergent literacy skills (Snow, Burns, & Griffin, 1998). In fact, spontaneously created or retold stories are the most accurate assessment of children's vocabulary, grammar, and sense of narrative construction; problems in this area are a good predictor of later academic difficulties.

Storytelling promotes **listening skills.** Listening comprehension is one of the skills most predictive of overall school performance and lifetime success. Summarizing the research in her book *Learning to Listen, Listening to Learn: Building Essential Skills in Young Children,* teacher and writer Mary Jalongo (2008) says listening is the language and literacy skill that develops earliest in young children and is practiced most frequently. As much as 80 percent of information is obtained through listening. Yet listening is the skill taught least frequently. By the end of high school, a student has had 12 years of formal training in writing, 6–8 years in reading, 1–2 years in speaking, and half a year or less in listening. Only 8 percent of instructional time is devoted to teaching listening.

Learning to listen may be harder than learning to read. Listeners must attend to verbal and nonverbal cues, while readers only have to pay attention to what is written (text and possibly pictures). For example, listeners must adjust to the speaker's pace, while readers can control their own pace. Readers can look back (review) or peek ahead (preview), while listeners must keep up with the ongoing flow of information. Printed text is fixed, whereas a speaker may shift content or style; reading is thus more "predictable" than listening. Information on the page has generally been edited down to its essentials *before* it reaches print. Oral language may meander, however, so it is only *after* the message is completed that the listener is able to sort out what is (not) relevant.

Balancing all these factors is not easy for adults. Imagine how much harder it is for a young child who has less experience figuring out where to focus! Pre-readers also have shorter attention spans and less memory capacity than readers, which makes listening even more difficult for preschoolers and early elementary children than older students. When teachers are asked about obstacles in the classroom, getting students to listen and focus their attention is high on the list. Yet teachers rarely receive training on how to help students develop these abilities. Employers also identify listening among the top three skills they seek in job applicants and a key determinant of promotions. Business organizations are more likely than schools to offer courses in listening.

Storytelling develops a ***positive self-identity.*** Through stories about their past experiences, children create autobiographical narratives and family histories (Nelson & Fivush, 2004). They can shape these stories to showcase emerging abilities and strong social networks. For example, their narratives can portray positive relationships with family members and friends or heroic examples of dealing with stress and conflict.

Storytelling helps children understand ***emotions.*** Storytelling is a safe place to process emotions. By preschool, most children can talk about four basic emotions: happy, sad, mad, and scared (Flavell & Miller, 1998). They begin to understand that emotions can result from interpersonal interactions, and storytelling is one way they can resolve internal psychological conflict about relationships with parents and siblings, teachers and peers. Older preschoolers can use puppets, dolls, and props in this context and create sophisticated narratives that demonstrate the complexity in their lives. In fact, research shows children are better at retelling stories when they use these concrete tools than when they use pictures from the narrative (Kim, 1999). Storytelling also helps children take on the perspective of others, thereby increasing their social knowledge and problem-solving abilities. Research confirms that perspective taking and narrative skills are linked (Curenton, 2006).

Storytelling promotes ***higher-order thinking skills.*** Early childhood researchers Mary Jane Moran and

Jennifer Jarvis (2001) note that stories can inspire young children to work with materials in more complex ways. Conversely, working with materials can inspire storytelling. They describe a group of preschoolers working with wire (beading, wrapping, bending) over a four-month period: "While working with wire, children began to tell stories that emerged from and became entwined with their sculptures. Creating with wire seemed to promote children's storytelling even as their stories stimulated ideas for wire sculptures. [The teacher] noticed that children stayed focused for longer and longer periods of time as their abilities to create stories with deliberateness flourished. No longer were they interested in simply...showing how they had made their wire sculptures. Children now focused on telling stories, which demonstrated their use of multiple perspectives and logical thinking.... One medium (wire) mediated their perceptions as they worked in the second medium (storytelling). The children's understanding of multiple perspectives in art also helped them develop the ability to distinguish between different qualities, attributes, or characteristics of other experiences or objects" (p. 33). For example, one child made a necklace out of wire and then dictated a story about a jewelry store and the King Moose buying the necklace for his wife. Several children combined their creations into a hanging sculpture and then drew it from various perspectives — from underneath or from the side. One child wrote this narrative beside his picture: *This is the wire sculpture and the ladder* (that the teacher stood on to hang it).

Likewise, storytelling itself can encourage multiple perspective-taking, as children consider the views of the different characters and the implications of unfolding events for their

Just as stories can inspire children to work with materials in more complex ways, working with materials can, in turn, inspire storytelling.

relationships with one another. Stories that take them just beyond the realm of their everyday experiences can encourage young children to approach life with their senses refreshed and open to new sights and sounds, events, and emotions. This phenomenon of enhancing perspective-taking can be especially useful in group activities that focus on topics in mathematics (exploring the properties of shapes from different angles), science (sorting and classifying natural objects by various attributes), or physical development (experiencing the body in different positions in space). Story starters are a natural lead-in to young children's explorations and discoveries in these and other areas.

Conclusion

"Listening to stories enables children to have fun with words and learn more about language," says early childhood specialist and writer Linda Ranweiler (2002, p. 59). Creating stories with preschoolers can be entertaining and instructive for adults too. Below is a summary of the benefits of storytelling with children:

- Builds vocabulary (introduces new words)

- Builds phonological awareness and recognition of language patterns

- Enhances ability to sustain conversations (extended discourse)

- Develops listening skills; increases attention span and concentration

- Promotes higher-order thinking skills and perspective-taking

- Contributes to overall school readiness and academic success

- Develops a sense of narrative including the elements of character, setting, dialogue, and plot

- Encourages inventing one's own stories which involves imagination and anticipation

- Encourages participation (contributing ideas, making predictions, and reacting to characters and events)

- Promotes a positive self-identify

- Provides a safe setting for exploring emotions

- Nurtures an understanding of human nature

- Develops a sense of empathy

- Develops a sense of humor

- Transmits family and cultural history

- Creates an awareness of other cultures

- Establishes a sense of community

Story starters, as one form of storytelling, can help to promote early development in all these ways. Children hear and use an increasingly rich vocabulary to carry out the activities inspired by the stories. They observe the diverse ways their peers use materials to take off on the initial narrative ideas, which in turn stimulates their own imaginative flights. As children work alongside one another, they talk about what they are doing, solve problems, help one another, and enjoy the dynamic interplay of conversation, materials, actions, and ideas. Story starters enable children to represent their thoughts and experiences, and to create new ones as they make a story their own.

3

Using Stories to Start Group Times

No doubt you have read stories to children. Perhaps you have also told them stories. You may have narrated a familiar fairytale, for example, or drawn on a story from a favorite book. Some adults enjoy making up tales, based on children's real experiences and interests, or inventing imaginary characters and events. You may even have created stories together with children, "co-narrating" with them as they contributed themes, characters, and scenarios. In each of these instances, the act of storytelling *is* the focus of the activity you share with them. That is, the story "stands alone" as a goal in and of itself.

Story Starters Versus Stand-Alone Stories

Story starters — our term for the very short stories used to begin group-time activities — have some features in common with these types of stand-alone storytelling, but also some distinct qualities. Both promote literacy, especially oral language skills such as vocabulary and comprehension. The main difference is that story starters are used to introduce an activity with its own purpose, rather than the story and its telling being the primary learning goal itself. Thus, story starters may be used to focus on any curriculum content area. Language and literacy are one obvious topic, but story starters can also provide a gateway to learning concepts and practicing skills in mathematics, science, physical development (motor skills), and the creative arts (art, pretend play, and movement and music).

In this chapter, we describe ten effective strategies for using story starters, including their similarities and differences with stand-alone storytelling. For additional information on general storytelling techniques, consult one of the many guides on sharing stories with young children available in print (e.g., Paley, 1990; Ranweiler, 2004; Trostle-Brand & Donato, 2001) and online (e.g., the National Storytelling Network; Storytelling Ring).

Ten Strategies for Effective Story Starters

1. Keep the story short.
In stand-alone stories, the beginning of the narrative leads to an elaboration of the story. Storytelling occupies the entire activity period. Story starters are shorter so children can quickly move to the content focus of group time and begin using the materials for the activity. For example, a storytelling activity might involve a long narrative about a child who travels to imaginary lands and discovers the different kinds of shoes people wear. The story might elaborate on the sizes, colors, shapes, textures, and styles of footwear, with children contributing observations about their own shoes or those they've seen in store windows, books, or the media. If this same idea is used as a story starter, it might be a brief tale about a child taking a walk, looking at the ground, and noticing everyone's shoes. If art were the focus, the teacher would immediately hand out drawing materials and encourage children to draw what they think such a child might see. As the children worked, they might develop on the same ideas and details that would emerge in the stand-alone story. However, the focus in the group-time activity would also be on children putting their ideas on paper, and transforming mental images into concrete representations. If it were a math activity, the concept of "two-ness" (pairs) might be explored. Children

might also tally the number of shoes, or pairs of shoes, they created. Or science might be the primary content area, as children pointed out similarities and differences in the attributes of the shoes they and their peers were drawing.

2. Keep the story simple.
As discussed in chapter 2, listening can be challenging, especially for young children (Jalongo, 2008). It

Telling a simple story helps children maintain their focus. In a story about shapes, for example, characters might wonder how the properties of a shape can help them solve a puzzle.

involves attending to many verbal and nonverbal elements at the same time, including words, sentence structure, sequencing of ideas, pacing of speech, tone of voice, facial gestures, and body movements. Preschoolers are easily distracted if they are bombarded with an excess of all these variables at once. Simplicity, like brevity, helps them maintain their focus and attend to the main ideas you want them to consider. For example, if the purpose of a small-group time is to explore shapes, the story starter should not involve an intense conflict in which two characters fight over who gets to play with a shape puzzle. Instead, tell a simple story where the characters wonder how the properties of a shape can help them solve the puzzle. To make it more interesting, you can have them disagree over whether to use the sides (edges) or the corners (angles) of a shape as a clue.

3. Follow a basic story structure.

Young children like stories with a clear and simple structure. According to children's book author Barbara Seuling, "Editors [of children's picture books] look for good, solid stories with beginnings, middles, and ends – a character and his dilemma; followed by the development, showing how that character manages to cope with his situation and change in some way to make it more acceptable; and a satisfying ending" (2007, p. 38). Keep this idea of a simple structure in mind as you create story starters too. For example, tell a straightforward narrative in which the character(s) face a dilemma, take part in the unfolding of the problem, and then resolve it. Or the story can set up the problem, and children can then use the materials to work out different solutions. For example, in a language and literacy small-group time, you might begin with a story about someone wanting to send a get-well card to a friend but not having paper and crayons. You could distribute other materials (large-print newspaper ads,

scissors, glue, pipe cleaners, old greeting cards, adhesive-backed letters, and so on) and invite the children to use these alternative items to make their cards. (Of course, children might choose to use the materials in other ways too.)

Another basic story structure is to have a character discover something (a new person, place, object, action, or event), learn about its properties, and use this knowledge in a novel way. Again, the story can lead into the children exploring materials or trying the actions described in the story, and making and applying their own discoveries. For example, a physical development large-group time might begin with a story about a child discovering different ways to cross a stream, depending on the width of the water at that spot. You could set up different "crossings" (for example, parallel strips of tape on the floor, separated by narrow, medium, and wide distances) and encourage children to try different movements (steps, jumps, spins, hops, leaps, swims) to go from one side to the other.

4. Plan and practice the story.

Storytelling can be planned and rehearsed, or done spontaneously to capture the moment. With story starters, however, it is best to know what you will say before group time begins. This preparation allows you to make the story work in service of the skills or concepts you want the children to explore. Neither you nor they will be distracted as you search for words to express the central ideas of the story or figure out the details as you go. Planning and practice makes it more likely

Ideas for story starters can be inspired by a variety of sources, including recurring themes in children's pretend play, the content area of a group-time activity, and children's interests and experiences.

that you will follow the guidelines of keeping the story short, simple, and structured. When your mind is not scrambling to find the next words, you can more easily focus on the children's input and the directions they might take the story's theme after you distribute the materials. Put simply, a smoothly told story starter will make for a smooth transition to the rest of the group-time activity.

5. Draw on multiple sources for story ideas.

Both storytelling and story starters can be inspired in many ways. They might be adapted from favorite and familiar storybooks you've read with the children. For example, "Goldilocks and the Three Bears" opens up possibilities for counting and ordering in mathematics, or the bears could have name labels on

their pillows to spark a language and literacy activity. You can also recount stories you've heard from other people or in other settings, including folk tales the children have encountered at home or in the community. Stories can emerge wholly created from your imagination, based on a play theme that is popular among the children. Recurring ideas in the pretend play of children in the HighScope Demonstration Preschool include kitties or puppies, going to the doctor, dinosaurs, birthday parties, and new babies in the house. At other times, children have introduced play themes derived from special interests and experiences with their families, such as camping, wrestling, kite flying, making movies (cinematography), gardening, and playing music in a rock band. Stories may also be motivated by a particular problem you want to help the children solve, for example, how they feel if the block structure they're building is knocked down when others run in the classroom.

In story starters, in particular, the theme can be inspired by the content area that is the focus of the group-time activity. In fact, most of the story starters presented in this book originated in just this way. The author thought about a skill or concept addressed in the HighScope Preschool Curriculum — such as recognizing and creating simple patterns — and then devised a story and an accompanying set of materials for children to explore this topic. The materials themselves may spark an idea. For example, if you have sets of paint chips so children can investigate color gradations, you might invent a story about a painter trying to decide how light or dark a shade to use on the outside of a house (seriation). Or, if your focus is science, and the effects of light and shadow, the story might be about what color the painter should choose for a house in an open field versus in a shaded forest. In addition to paint chips, the materials might include flashlights and dark sheets of construction paper to cover the beams.

6. Make the story open-ended.

While all interactive storytelling encourages children to contribute to characterization and plot, it is especially important for story starters to be a jumping off point for children's independent explorations and discoveries. The more open-ended the story, the more children can build on its

Story starters should be a lead-in to children's independent explorations — that is, children should be free to use materials and make discoveries in their own way.

underlying premise to use the materials creatively and construct their own ideas. For example, in a literacy activity focused on concepts about print, you might tell a story about children visiting a house where there aren't any books, so they decide to write their own. You would then distribute book-making materials and leave it to the children to come up with their own story themes, characters, ways of "writing" text, illustrations, and so on.

As in all small- and large-group activities, regardless of how they are introduced, it is important that children be free to use materials and explore ideas in their own way. Whether you begin with a story starter or another opening strategy, the five ingredients of active participatory learning — materials, manipulation, choice, child language and thought, and adult scaffolding — should always be present. (See chapter 4 for more information on HighScope's general guidelines for group times and applying the principles of active learning.)

7. Use the story to build children's vocabulary.

Storytelling is one of the most effective ways to grow the number of words young children have in their receptive and expressive repertoire. To build vocabulary with story starters, use the following strategies:

Introduce a few new words in each story starter. Depending on the focus of the activity, use appropriate content-related words to describe the materials, your actions with them, and/or the results the actions produce. For example, in an art appreciation story about buying postcard reproductions at the museum, you might use

words such as *shading, brush stroke,* or *background.*

Invite children to share what they observe. As they begin to work with materials, encourage children to use their own words to describe their actions and observations. Ask them to relate and compare what they do and see to what occurred in the story. For example, in a science activity, ask whether their investigations produce the same or different results than those experienced by the characters. Invite them to give you directions to reproduce their results. Encourage children to provide descriptive details.

Use familiar synonyms and simple definitions and examples. To help children understand new vocabulary words, accompany them with other words the children already know and familiar examples that illustrate their meaning. For example, a physical development activity story might include the words *spinning* or *rotating.* You can help children learn these new words by relating them to *turning* or *going around in a circle* — terms they already know — and by demonstrating the action with your body or the materials used in the activity.

Connect words to children's gestures and ideas. In addition to introducing words during the story itself, the direction in which the children take off from the tale will provide many opportunities for adding new words to their vocabularies. For example, if a pretend-play story involves a trip to an imaginary place, you can attach emotion words they are less familiar with (e.g., *scary, exciting, brave*) to the scenarios they contribute to the tale.

*Use words to issue intriguing challenges or pose **What if...** questions.* Midway through group time, after children have explored materials and ideas in various ways, encourage them to consider possibilities that expand or change the direction of the story starter. For example, you might follow up a mathematics story starter about bunnies having a race by saying, *I wonder if you can go twice as fast as those rabbits!*

Continue to use the words you introduce in story starters. Hearing a word once is not enough for young children to add it to their vocabularies. They need to hear words repeated, and in different contexts, before they can understand and incorporate them in their own speech. For example, to follow up a music story starter, you can *chant* or *hum* during transitions (using these words to describe those behaviors), comment on the *loudness* or *softness* of their voices as children roleplay during work time, refer to the *trill* of a bird at outside time, or do a planning or recall activity based on different vocal *pitches.*

For more ideas on encouraging child talk and enhancing children's vocabularies, see the adult-child interaction strategies described in *Educating Young Children: Active Learning Practices for Preschool and Child Care Programs* (Hohmann, Weikart, & Epstein, 2008), *Essentials of Active Learning in Preschool: Getting to Know the HighScope Curriculm* (Epstein, 2007a), and *HighScope Step by Step: Lesson Plans for the First 30 Days* (Marshall, Lockhart, & Fewson, 2007).

8. Connect stories to materials.

Access to individual or shared materials is a hallmark of most group times (see chapter 4), so it is important to make an explicit link between the story starter and the materials (if any) to be used in the activity. To do so, you can use the materials as you tell the story, refer to them in the narrative, and/or introduce them immediately after the short tale is completed with a statement that links them to the story. For example, in a music activity about *loud* and *quiet* noises, use simple percussion instruments to make the corresponding sounds as you share the opening story. Refer to characters, actions, or settings as *noisy* or *quiet.* Distribute instruments or other noisemakers during or after the story so children can explore the contrasts on their own.

9. Be moderately expressive in telling the story.

Storytelling with children benefits from vocal range, hand and body gestures, and facial expressions. With stand-alone stories, these strategies help to draw children into the drama and get them involved as participants in (re)telling the story and acting out the scenes. With story starters, while you also want to engage children in the activity, you don't want the story and its dramatization to overshadow the activity that follows. In choosing vocal and gestural expressions to emphasize, therefore, opt for those that call attention to the materials or their manipulation, that is, the activity elements that are the content focus of the group time.

It is important that teachers explicitly link the story starter to any materials that will be used in the activity. Teachers can use or refer to the materials during or at the end of the narrative.

For example, if children at large-group time will be exploring the concepts *up* and *down* through creative body movements, you might start with a story about an elevator that went up and down, using your body movements accordingly, without also exaggerating the high and low pitch of your voice or waving your arms high and low. You can introduce these other elements later, or in a subsequent group-time activity, but for "starters," limit your voice and gestures to the primary concept(s) you want children to explore.

10. Be sensitive to children's varying levels of engagement with the story.

In stand-alone storytelling, the adult's aim is to actively engage all the children with the narrative itself. Your interaction strategies will therefore include extended discourse — one-on-one and group-level — to encourage children to elaborate on their ideas and to link them to the story's themes and characters (see Dickinson & Tabors, 2002, discussed in chapter 2). When the story is only used as a starter, however, children may become engaged in the activity in ways that have nothing to do with the opening narrative. To be consistent with the HighScope approach and good developmental practice in general, it is important to follow each child's lead and not force explorations and interactions to fit within the parameters set out in the story.

For example, following the opening story, children may simply be engrossed in exploring materials and tools, experimenting with their voices, or moving their bodies in different ways. They may (not) describe what they are doing and seeing as they continue to work. In fact, as in any group or work-time activity, children may be so intent on their actions and observations that interrupting them with story-related conversation will halt their active learning. Therefore, as with all interactions, follow each child's lead as he or she engages with the activity, whether or not it follows the story. (Again, see Epstein, 2007a, and Hohmann, Weikart, & Epstein, 2008, for appropriate scaffolding strategies that match children's personal learning styles and developmental levels.)

4

Conducting Effective Group Times

Before making story starters a part of group-time activities, it is important to understand the general principles and practices for conducting effective small- and large-group times. The strategies listed below are those implemented in settings using the HighScope Preschool Curriculum, but they can be applied in any developmentally based program serving young children.

Overview of Small- and Large-Group Times

Like many early childhood programs, HighScope has a set time in the daily routine when a group of children, typically 6–10, meet with an adult for a shared small-group activity. There is also a consistent time during the day when the entire class of 16–20 children gathers with the adults for a large-group activity.

Small-group time lasts 10–15 minutes, although if children are engaged it might extend to 20 minutes. Each classroom teacher meets with the same group of children on a consistent basis; group members are the same as those with whom the teacher meets for planning, recall, and snacktimes and mealtimes. They gather at a designated place, such as a table or area rug, to participate in a teacher-initiated, hands-on learning experience. Adults use this time to introduce new materials, ideas, and activities and explore these alongside the children. Small-group time gives teachers an opportunity to observe and interact daily with the same group of children and provides children with regular peer contact and interactions. This consistency strengthens relationships and creates a supportive educational environment that supports and extends the learning experiences children have during the other parts of the day.

Large-group time is the part of the day when everyone participates in an activity together. Like small-group time, large-group time typically lasts 10–15 minutes. All the children and adults in the classroom come together to share music and movement activities, storytelling, or reenacting stories and nursery rhymes. These gatherings contribute to the sense of community in the classroom. Large-group times require a space with enough room for every child and adult to move freely and vigorously during the activity. Programs with enough physical space may have a permanent gathering area, such as a rug in the middle of the room. In smaller facilities, adults may have to move equipment aside to create this space, for example, moving lightweight storage baskets with handles to the room's outer edges. In warm climates or seasons, the class may gather outside under a tree or on a patio.

HighScope teachers put thought and effort into planning group times. Although adults initiate group times around specific content, they base them on their daily observations of children's wide-ranging interests, encourage children to make choices about how they use the materials, and talk with children about what they are doing and learning. Group times also offer all children the chance to interact with others. This experience is especially important for those who choose to play alone during work (choice) time. Because group times are unpressured, even shy or solitary children can participate in ways that feel comfortable to them.

Applying Active Participatory Learning at Group Times

Across the range of early childhood programs, children's experiences at group times can vary greatly. At one end of the spectrum, children's activities may be highly controlled and directed by the teacher (for example, listening to an academic-style lesson or copying a specific motor skill). At the other end, children might simply be given some materials to explore or be allowed to run free without any adult guidance or support.

HighScope takes a balanced approach. During group times, children and adults both play an active role in the learning process. That is, small- and large-group times are adult-initiated activities in which children are encouraged to explore materials and ideas in their own way, with adults sharing the excitement of the children's discoveries and scaffolding their learning. To guarantee that children of all developmental and ability levels have a positive learning experience during group times, HighScope teachers apply the same *five ingredients of active participatory learning* that are used throughout the rest of the program day.

Materials. Programs offer abundant supplies of diverse and age-appropriate materials. Materials are chosen to appeal to all the senses. They are also open ended, that is, they lend themselves to being used in a variety of ways so they can introduce children to new experiences and stimulate their

During small-group time, teachers observe and interact daily with the same group of children. This consistency provides children with regular peer contact and interactions, and creates a supportive environment for learning.

thinking. At group times, attention to this active-learning component means children encounter many types of materials, including some they might not choose to play with on their own. Group times offer an opportunity to introduce new materials — or reintroduce old materials — to the classroom. Depending on the activity, children are each given their own set of materials to work with and/or they are provided with easy access to shared materials. In some activities, such as a large-group movement or singing activity, there may be no "materials" other than the children's own bodies or voices.

Manipulation. Children handle, examine, combine and transform materials and ideas. They make discoveries through direct hands-on and "minds-on" contact with these resources. At group times, the emphasis on manipulation means children experience materials directly, that is, they examine the physical properties of objects, handle things, listen to and make sounds, move their bodies, feel different textures, smell different aromas, taste different foods, and interact one-on-one and in a group context with peers and adults.

Choice. In an active learning setting, children have opportunities to make choices throughout the day. They choose materials and play partners, create and develop play ideas, and plan activities according to their interests. The value of child choice during group times means children are free to explore materials and ideas in ways that are meaningful to them. They are not expected to use materials in a prescribed way or produce specific products determined by an adult. Teachers provide the materials, but children choose how to use them.

Child language and thought. Children describe what they are doing and what they understand about their experiences. They communicate verbally and nonverbally as they think about their behavior and modify their conclusions to take new learning into account. During group times, children talk about their actions and reflect on their observations as they interact with materials and one another. Adults gain insight into how children understand and interpret the world by taking careful note of what the children say and do.

Adult scaffolding. Adults support children's current level of understanding, while challenging them to advance to the next stage of thinking and reasoning. In this way, adults help children gain knowledge, develop creative problem-solving skills, and reflect on what they are learning. As group time unfolds, teachers circulate among the children, supporting and extending their individual explorations and discoveries. They observe and imitate children's actions, repeat the words

Although group times are initiated by adults, both adults and children play an active role in the learning process. Children independently explore materials and ideas as adults share children's discoveries and scaffold their learning.

they use to extend children's vocabularies, and pose open-ended questions that encourage children to try new things and consider the "what, how, and why" of their experiences. Adults also refer children to one another to share ideas and solve problems collaboratively.

In sum, when applied to group times, the five ingredients of active learning translate into adult support for children exploring materials, experimenting, building, creating and solving problems in their own ways. Young children talk about what they are doing and seeing, make discoveries, and share ideas with others. As a result, group experiences spark many ideas that children extend throughout the program day and often carry into their thoughts and actions outside of school. Group times thus serve as a springboard for development.

Carrying Out Group Activities

When planning and preparing for group times, teachers think about the *beginning* of the session, that is, how they will introduce ideas and distribute the materials. They think about the *middle,* or how they will support and extend — scaffold — children's learning. And they think about the *end,* that is, how they will bring the activity to a close, clean up materials, and transition to the next part of day's routine.

- *Beginning.* Children arrive eager to begin work, so teachers engage them as soon as they arrive at the gathering place. At this point the teacher may use a story starter or make a brief introductory statement to connect the activity to children's interests, introduce the materials (which often are new or unfamiliar to children), and/or focus children on a particular content area. The teacher then hands out the materials (if she has not done this already) and encourages children to begin working.

- *Middle.* Once children have begun to work with the materials (including sounds and movements), the teacher's role is to pay attention to their actions and ideas, scaffold further learning, and encourage them to interact with and learn from one another. Adults do this by closely attending to each child, getting down on their level, watching and listening to them, imitating and building on their actions, conversing with children and following their leads, asking questions sparingly, encouraging children to solve problems, and referring them to one another for ideas and assistance. Teachers also support children's highly individual use of materials, and their observations about what they are doing and learning. In fact, one indication of an effective group time is the sheer variety of ideas the children initiate!

- *End.* Letting children know when group time is about to end, with a two- or three-minute warning, gives them control over how to bring the session to closure. Some may be ready to stop, others may want to work a bit longer, and still others may want to store what they are doing to continue using the materials at work (choice) time. So, while each group time has a predetermined ending, teachers schedule time throughout the day for transitions so children can move from one segment to the next as they are ready. Children help to gather and put away the materials. Adults also remind children where the materials from group time are stored so they know they are available and accessible for further use.

Follow-up to group-time activities is also important. Children — and teachers — emerge from group times with many ideas about how to continue and extend the excitement and learning that occurred during an activity. Based on teachers' observations of children and what they see and hear from them, teachers may add new materials to the classroom, plan related group activities, use part of the activity as a basis for a planning or recall strategy, or take an idea and use it as the spark for an engaging transition. Successful group times inspire children to continue using the materials and exploring the ideas in additional ways during work (choice) time or other parts of the daily routine. Parents can provide comparable materials and experiences with their children at home as well, thereby extending the learning even further.

This book will help you incorporate all the ingredients of active learning and effective group times as you use story starters with the children in your program. Each activity plan identifies the content area addressed, briefly describes what children do and learn, lists the materials needed, presents the story starter for beginning the activity, suggests strategies to scaffold children's learning (including vocabulary words to use in conversation), and offers follow-up ideas to extend learning throughout the classroom and other parts of the program day. Using this activity plan as a guideline, you can plan and carry out group-time activities with the story starters you create on your own. (For guidelines on creating your own story starters, see chapters 12 and 13.)

For more information on planning and conducting group times in HighScope programs, see *Essentials of Active Learning in Preschool: Getting to Know the HighScope Curriculum* (Epstein, 2007a); *Educating Young Children: Active Learning Practices for Preschool and Child Care Programs:* (Hohmann, Weikart, & Epstein, 2008); *HighScope Step by Step: Lesson Plans for the First 30 Days* (Marshall, Lockhart, & Fewson, 2007); *Small-Group Times to Scaffold Early Learning* (Epstein, Gainsley, Lockhart, Marshall, Neill, & Rush, 2009); and *50 Large-Group Activities for Active Learners* (Boisvert & Gainsley, 2006).

PART TWO: STORY STARTER ACTIVITIES

5

Language, Literacy, and Communication

The story starters in Language, Literacy, and Communication will help children learn about these key topics:

- *Phonological awareness* — Hearing and making the sounds of language, including rhymes and alliteration

- *Concepts about print* — Understanding how books and other printed materials work

- *Comprehension* — Understanding the meaning of words, conversations, and stories

- *Alphabet knowledge* — Recognizing, reading, and writing letters and simple words

Get Well Soon

1

Content area:
Language, Literacy, and Communication

Time of day:
Small-group time

Materials
For each child and teacher: Paper and writing materials (e.g., crayons, markers, colored pencils, chalk)

To share: Letters of the alphabet; sample words, such as *Get Well Soon*, for children to copy

For backup: Envelopes (e.g., blank and samples from junk mail); extra paper and writing tools

What Children Do and Learn

Children make "Get-Well" cards for sick teddy bears to practice writing skills and become familiar with a form of environmental print.

Story Starter

Josh was eager to go to Teddy Bear Preschool and play with his friend Drema. But Josh began to wheeze and sneeze, and whiffle and sniffle. He was sick and had to stay home. Next day, Drema couldn't go to school either because she began to wheeze and sneeze, and whiffle and sniffle. Soon, all the other teddy bears began to wheeze and… (pause for children to fill in the refrain). *Everyone had to stay home so no one was left to send get-well cards.* Distribute the materials and say *Suppose we send them get-well cards to help them feel better soon.*

Scaffolding Children's Learning

Encourage children to make get-well cards. If children explore the materials rather than use them to make cards, talk about what they are doing. Discuss the get-well pictures they draw and the letters and words they write. If asked, help them fold the paper and write their messages. If children want to "mail" their cards, talk about what is usually written on an envelope (names and addresses). Provide envelopes from junk mail as examples. Encourage them to use the letters and sample words to trace or copy, and to identify letters or words by sound. Refer children to one another for help (e.g., Better *begins with the /b/ sound, the same as in* Becky. *Maybe she can show you how she writes the first letter in her name*).

Vocabulary words: *eager, feel better, get-well card, send, sniffle, wheeze*

Follow-up Ideas

Provide paper and writing tools, and encourage children to make written props for their role play (e.g., *Will you send invitations to your party? What will you use to make a card for the baby doll in the hospital?*) Write individual or group thank you notes to people who hosted or guided the class on a field trip. If children are interested, make a mailbox (e.g., slit the top of a shoe box) where they can post their letters. Provide old greetings cards and junk mail for children to use in their role play.

Giant's Birthday Party

2

What Children Do and Learn

Children make up the names of guests to invite to a party to explore words that begin with the same letter sounds (alliteration).

Content area:
Language, Literacy, and Communication

Time of day:
Small-group time

Materials
For each child and teacher: None

To share: Chart paper and markers

For backup: Drawing materials (e.g., paper, markers, crayons)

Story Starter

A giant named Blue Beastie was having a birthday party and he wanted to invite friends whose names began with the same sound as his, the /b/ sound. He wrote a list, beginning with the names Brave Betty and Bouncing Ben. Who else should Blue Beastie put on his party list? What other names can we think of that start with the /b/ sound? Solicit children's ideas and write them down on chart paper. Note if any of the children's or teachers' names begin with /b/. Take several suggestions for names, then continue: *There was another giant named Shiny Shelley. She invited Short Sheila and Sharp Sheldon to her party. Their names begin with the /sh/ sound. Who else should Shiny Shelley invite?* Comment on children's or teachers' names that begin with the /sh/ sound.

Scaffolding Children's Learning

After the children add /sh/ names, encourage them to suggest different names for giants and add names to a party list with the same initial letter sound. Children may choose their own names and/or words that begin with the same sound as their name. Give every child who wants a chance to suggest a giant's name for the party list. If children suggest a name that does not belong (e.g., a *J* name when the category is *H*), do not correct them, but say something like *Joshua can go on a party list with Jolly Jason and Jingly Jessica.* Encourage children to write letters and names on the chart paper. Distribute drawing materials if they want to make pictures of the giants, guests, parties, or make other drawings of their choice.

Vocabulary words: *bouncing, invite, letter, list, same sound, shiny, sharp*

Follow-up Ideas

Provide materials for children to draw and write party lists and invitations at work (choice) time. Draw and write party invitations at small-group time. Encourage children to make up alliterative additions to their names or actions at transition times (e.g., *Merry Marijata hopped to the rug; Janelle jumped to the rug; How about you Sam? I wonder if you'll do something with the /s/ sound*).

3 "Just Right"

Content area:
Language, Literacy, and Communication

Time of day:
Small-group time

Materials
For each child and teacher: 10–15 letters made of wood, plastic, heavy cardboard, or foam

To share: Extra letters

For backup: Paper and writing materials (to trace and copy letters)

What Children Do and Learn
Children describe and compare the look and sounds of letters and choose the one that is "just right," based on its attributes. (It helps if children are familiar with the story "Goldilocks and the Three Bears." You may want to read or tell this story the day before you do this activity.)

Story Starter
Goldilocks sat at the Three Bears' letter table. She said, "I'm looking for a letter that has only straight lines." She picked up the letter O *and said, "This* O *is round." Then she picked up the letter* B *and said, "This* B *is straight and curved." She picked up the letter* A *and said, "This* A *is just right. It has only straight lines."* With the children, trace the outlines of the letters and talk about their straight and curved parts. Repeat this process with three other letters, looking for those with straight-only, curved-only, and straight and curved parts. Give each child a set of letters and say *I wonder which letters will be "just right" for you.*

Scaffolding Children's Learning
Talk to the children about what they think is (or is not) "just right" about the letters they choose without correcting them when they make mistakes in describing the letters. Encourage them to invent other bases for comparing the letters, such as their size, shape, number of holes or circles, number or length of straight lines, sound, relationship to familiar words (whether they share a first letter or last letter). For example, say *This* I *is too skinny, this* B *is too fat, but this* C *is just right* or H, *the /h/ sound, isn't in my name,* M, *the /m/ sound isn't in my name, but* K, *the /k/ sound, for* Kendra, *sounds just right.* For children who are just beginning to explore letters, describe their properties, and help them name the letters and say their sounds. Encourage children who are interested to trace and copy letters.

Vocabulary words: *curved, just right, loop, outline, round, straight*

Follow-up Ideas

As children work with letters (reading, tracing, copying, writing), encourage them to describe and compare characteristics related to appearance and sounds. For example, children may explore whether letters have straight lines or curves or whether they are open or closed (e.g., *C* versus *O*). Also, encourage children to "listen" to letters that make "hard" or "soft" sounds (e.g., *K* versus *S*), and to look at and feel how their mouths move when saying different letters (e.g., lips opened on *A* versus closed on *M*). Children can use mirrors to see how their own mouths move and observe one another.

Encourage children to explore and compare different letters based on characteristics such as size, shape, number of "holes" or circles, and whether their lines are straight or curved.

4 Letter Land Express

Content area:
Language, Literacy, and Communication

Time of day:
Small-group time

Materials
For each child and teacher: Train track made of strips of paper; small block (or other object to serve as a train); 6–10 letters including the first letter in his or her name and other familiar names and words (for younger children, begin with 3–5 letters)

To share: Additional letters; extra lengths of track

For backup: Props for places such as towns or farms (e.g., blocks of different sizes to serve as buildings, pieces of fabric to serve as grass or bodies of water, people and animal figures)

What Children Do and Learn
Children find letters along a train track made of paper and invent the names of places that begin with that letter.

Story Starter
Spread several letters on your track and say *Choo choo. The Letter Land Express is whistling and chugging down the train track.* Move your train along the track. Encourage children to make train sounds. *It's stopping at different places along the way.* Stop the train at a letter, pick it up, and say *It's the letter S and it makes the /s/ sound. This must be where Samantha lives.* Put the letter down and move your train to another letter. Pick it up and encourage (or help) the children to name it (for example, *D*) and say, *It's the letter D and it makes the /d/ sound. Who do you suppose lives here?* Ask for the children's ideas. Give each child a train track, a train, and a set of letters, and say *I wonder what letters your train will stop at.*

Scaffolding Children's Learning
Name, and encourage children to name, the letters and their sounds. Encourage them to think of people (e.g., themselves, classmates, family members), objects (e.g., toys), or places (e.g., areas of the room) whose names begin with that letter. Accept both real words and nonsense (invented) words. Encourage children to help one another find letters (e.g., *John wants his train to stop where the cat lives. He says he needs a* C. *Who can help him find one?*) If children just explore driving their train along the track, say *I wonder if you'll stop at any letters.* Help them search for and name familiar letters.

Vocabulary words: beginning sound, chugging, express, letter sound, whistling

Follow-up Ideas

At large-group time, have children move around the room along a track (for example, squares of paper) with large letters written on the squares. When you say *Stop,* children do a movement that begins with the letter they are standing on (for example, they may choose to *march* if they are on the letter *M*). Begin with letters that are associated with movements familiar to the children (e.g., *W* for *walk* or *H* for *hop*). You can use music to start and stop movement around the track, or have children take turns saying when to stop. Children can also take turns choosing a movement to match their letter and having others in the class imitate them. Help and encourage children to name the letters and sounds, and emphasize the beginning sound in the movement they choose (e.g., *Nettie landed on* S *which makes the /s/ sound. She says to* swing *our arms*).

5 Lost Letters

Content area:
Language,
Literacy, and
Communication

Time of day:
Small-group time

Materials
*For each child
and teacher:* Basket
(or other small
container); 6–10
letters (e.g., wood,
plastic, cardboard)

To share: Additional
letters, several of
each spread around
the table

For backup: Paper
and writing tools
(e.g., markers,
pencils, crayons) to
trace or copy letters

What Children Do and Learn

Children choose, name, and say the sounds of letters as they put them back in a basket. (It helps if children are familiar with "Little Red Riding Hood." You may want to read or tell this story the day before you do this activity.)

Story Starter

Little Red Riding Hood walked through the woods to Grandma's house with a basketful of letters to give her as a present. Choose several letters. Name them with the children and say their sounds. *On the way, Little Red Riding Hood met the Big Bad Wolf. She was so scared when the wolf growled at her that she dropped her basket and all the letters fell out.* Dump the letters on the table. *After Grandma gave her a mug of hot chocolate and a hug, she felt courageous again. She returned to the woods and put all the letters back in her basket.* Give each child a basket of letters, spread more letters on the table, and say *I wonder what letters you will find to put in your baskets.*

Teachers can use comments and questions to encourage children to connect letters in their baskets to the beginning letter and sound of familiar words.

Scaffolding Children's Learning

Talk about the letters children put in their baskets. Name, and encourage them to name, the letters and their sounds. Use comments and questions to help children connect letters to the beginning letter and sound of familiar words, such as their names (e.g., *You chose /c/ for* Carl), things they play with (*Yes,* P *sounds like the /p/ in* pegboard), colors and shapes (e.g., *It's* R *like the /r/ in your* red *shirt*), or parts of the daily routine (e.g., *Can you help me find a* G *for* group *time? It makes the /g/ sound*). If children are interested, encourage them to match letters, trade letters with one another, combine letters into words, and trace or copy letters.

Vocabulary words: *basketful, courageous, growl, letter, mug, scared, woods*

Follow-up Ideas

At planning and recall time, spread letters on the table and ask children to choose a letter for the area of the room or a material they will (did) play in or with. For children who are not yet capable, help them choose a letter that fits what they say. For example, if Shelby says she plans to play in the house area, you can say, *House begins with* H *and it makes the /h/ sound.* Then help Shelby find the letter *H.*

6 Not Again!

Content area:
Language, Literacy, and Communication

Time of day:
Small-group time

Materials
For each child and teacher: Strips of heavy-duty paper or tag board (approximately 2"–3" x 6"–8")

To share: Writing, drawing, and decorating materials and tools (e.g., markers, crayons, stickers, stamps and inkpads, yarn, scissors, tape, glue)

For backup: Books from the classroom library; extra strips of paper and decorating materials

What Children Do and Learn
Children explore the idea that some books are too long to read in one session and make bookmarks to mark their place.

Story Starter
The queen read a bedtime story to the prince that began "Once upon a time, a bear strolled in the woods. He ate the apples on the apple tree and fell asleep. When he woke up…" The prince interrupted, saying "I'm tired. Let's continue the story tomorrow." And he went to sleep too. The next day, the queen read to the prince again: "Once upon a time, a bear strolled in the woods. He ate the apples on the apple tree and fell asleep. When he woke up…" The prince said, "Not again! You read that yesterday. Read the next *part." What can the queen and prince do to help the queen know where to begin the next part of the story?* Talk about the children's ideas, ask if they have ever seen someone use a bookmark, and pass out materials for them to make bookmarks.

Scaffolding Children's Learning
Encourage children to share their ideas for solving the problem. Drawing on the children's experiences, talk about how the prince might feel annoyed or frustrated when he hears the same part of the story again. Help children who are interested write their letter links or other letters and words on their bookmarks. Talk about their drawings and other decorations. Encourage children to put bookmarks in books they would like to read at greeting time or work (choice) time the next day. For storybook collections, discuss how each story starts on a new page and how bookmarks can indicate where their favorite stories begin.

Vocabulary words: bedtime, bookmark, continue, stroll, tomorrow, yesterday

Follow-up Ideas
Encourage children to use bookmarks to note their favorite pictures or sections of a book, or their choice in the class song book to sing at large-group time. At planning and recall, encourage them to use bookmarks to indicate which books they will (or did) read at work (choice) time. At greeting, work, or small-group time, read books that last more than one session, and encourage children to mark the stopping place. Encourage children to take their bookmarks home to use themselves or to give as gifts for parents and older siblings.

Popsicle Letters

7

What Children Do and Learn
Children make letters with Popsicle sticks.

Story Starter
One day the refrigerator in the ice cream truck broke down and the Popsicles started to melt in the sun. "Hurry home," the truck driver said to the children, "and bring back cups and spoons. I'll give you free Popsicle soup to eat!" The children fetched cups and spoons and ate strawberry and lemon Popsicle soup. Talk about other flavors the children like. *But when they slurped up the last drop of soup, empty Popsicle sticks lay on the ground. Some sticks were next to each other and made letters.* Make and name a few letters using two or three sticks (e.g., *L, T, H,* or *K*). *The children decided to see what other letters they could make.* Give each child a set of Popsicle sticks and say *I wonder what letters you can make with your Popsicle sticks.*

Content area:
Language, Literacy, and Communication

Time of day:
Small-group time

Materials
For each child and teacher: 10 Popsicle sticks

To share: Written or 3-D letters for children to refer to and copy; extra Popsicle sticks

For backup: Paper and glue if children want to glue their Popsicle letters onto a paper; pipe cleaners or other bendable materials for children to make curved letters

Children use Popsicle sticks to make letters in their names, area signs, and other familiar words.

Scaffolding Children's Learning

Talk about the letters children make, including those in their names, area signs, and other familiar words (e.g., *mom, dad, cat, toy*). If they use the sticks without making letters, point out similarities to letters (e.g., *You made a row of sticks. They look like this part of the* L). Refer children to written and 3-D letters to copy and compare to the Popsicle letters. Encourage them to name and produce the sounds of the letters, and to think of other words beginning with the same letters. Ask them to help you make specific letters (e.g., *Can you help me make an* M *like in my name,* Mary. *How many sticks will I need?*).

Vocabulary words: *fetch, flavor, lemon, melt, Popsicle, refrigerator, slurped, strawberry*

Follow-up Ideas

Decide with the children where to store the leftover Popsicle sticks to use at work (choice) time. At small-group time, make letters with other materials, such as pipe cleaners, yarn, and twigs. Make a "Popsicle Letter Book" and put it in the book area. Read other alphabet books with the children. At planning (or recall time), give children Popsicle sticks to make a letter in the name of an area (or material) they will (or did) use at work (choice) time.

Rhyme Time

8

What Children Do and Learn

Children listen to simple verses and move in different ways, depending on whether or not the last word rhymes with the end word in the previous lines(s). (This activity works best after children have had practice rhyming individual words.)

Content area:
Language, Literacy, and Communication

Time of day:
Large-group time

Materials
For each child and teacher: None

To share: Carpet squares spread on the floor (two more squares than the number of children and adults)

For backup: None

Story Starter

Brown Town had a poetry contest. When the ending words in a poem rhymed, everyone had to crawl to another carpet square. But if the words didn't rhyme, they had to stay right where they were. Make sure each child is standing on a carpet square, and say *Here's the first poem. "I opened a book. And I saw a hook." Do you think the people in Brown Town crawled to another square or stayed where they were. If you think* book *and* hook *rhyme, crawl to another square.* Give children time to move. *Here's the next poem. "I opened a book. And I saw a fish." Book and fish. Will you crawl to another square or stay on the same one?*

Scaffolding Children's Learning

After one or two repeats, encourage children to supply the last word. Accept real words and made-up (nonsense) words. Make comments such as *I wonder if you'll rhyme this time or not* or *Will you try to trick us?* Expect some children to move at random or look to their peers for cues. Do not correct individual children, but comment on rhymes and movements for the class as a whole (e.g., *We're moving.* Cook *rhymes with* book). After children have had practice with the activity, make an occasional mistake (e.g., crawl on a non-rhyme or stay in place on a rhyme) and see if they correct you. If not, say *I don't think I did that right. Can you help me?*

Vocabulary words: *another, crawl, ending words, poem, poetry, rhyme*

Follow-up Ideas

Use rhymes at transitions (e.g., *If your name rhymes with* shoe, *go to the snack table.* Sue *and* Stu *both rhyme with* shoe. *If the end of your name rhymes with* head, *go to the snack table. There goes* Ed. Read books featuring rhyming, such as those by Dr. Seuss. When children are familiar with the book, stop now and then and encourage them to fill in the last word or phrase. Recite familiar poems and chants and encourage children to make up different rhyming endings (e.g., *Row, row, row your boat/Gently down the lake/Merrily, merrily, merrily, merrily/Life is but a _____*). Accept and have fun with children's real and made-up answers.

9 Street Fair

Content area:
Language, Literacy, and Communication

Time of day:
Small-group time

Materials
For each child and teacher: Strip of paper at least 12" tall x 24" wide; writing materials (e.g., crayons, markers, colored pencils); space to spread out on the floor (or tape paper to the wall at children's drawing height)

To share: Paper with some of the words children might want to write or copy (e.g., *street, fair, race, art, book, food, snow cone, pay, ticket*); letters they can copy or trace (e.g., wood, plastic, cardboard); extra strips of paper

For backup: Materials to hang banners (e.g., hole punch, string, tape)

What Children Do and Learn
Children write words and draw pictures on banners to advertise events for a street fair.

Story Starter
Eliot was excited. Tomorrow his town was having a big street fair. [If the children are more familiar with a carnival, circus, or similar event, substitute a word they know.] *As he and his family walked downtown, they saw banners saying where each event would happen. One banner said* Running Race *and had a picture of sneakers. Another banner advertised* Food Booths *with drawings of pizzas and ice cream cones. There were also banners for an art show, a book tent, and dancers.* Talk about banners the children have seen and what was written and drawn on them. Distribute the strips of paper and drawing materials, and make sure each child has ample work space. Say *I wonder what you will write and draw on your banners.*

Scaffolding Children's Learning
Talk with the children about the events they represent on their banners. Discuss the words they use to label each event and their illustrations of the activities and materials involved. Accept that some children will just scribble or draw on the page, some will write letters or words, and some will both write and draw. Support each child's efforts. When asked, help children write letters and spell words. Connect the letters and words they want to write to those they already know (e.g., Booth *starts with the /b/ sound, the same letter,* B, *that begins your name, Brett).* Encourage the children to help one another.

Provide children with sturdy letters they can copy or trace to write the words on their "Street Fair" banners.

Vocabulary words: advertise, banner, booth, downtown, event, street fair

Follow-up Ideas

Use the banners to act out the events at small- and large-group times. Encourage children to assemble dress-up clothes, and provide materials for them to make props related to each type of event. Ask children what other events they want to act out and how to represent them in pictures and words on banners.

10 Traffic Jam

Content area:
Language,
Literacy, and
Communication

Time of day:
Small-group time

Materials
For each child and teacher: Toy figures of people (at least 2 apiece) and animals (at least 4 apiece); toy vehicles (at least 2 apiece)

To share: Extra figures and vehicles that can be used to represent people and vehicles on the street; materials to create stores, roads, and so on (e.g., toy stop signs, small blocks); paper and writing tools

For backup: None

What Children Do and Learn
Children act out and add to a story narrative using toy figures and other props.

Story Starter
There was a lot of traffic on Main Street. Grown-ups rushed to work, parents dropped off their children at preschool, and trucks delivered food to the supermarket. Move several figures around. *What else do you think was happening on the busy street?* Talk about and act out the children's ideas. As you continue to move the figures, say *Suddenly a parade of animals came marching down the street. The circus was in town! Traffic came to a halt.* Stop moving the figures. *People honked because they didn't want to be late to where they were going. The animals were scared and confused by the noise. The police officer said, "We have a problem. What can we do?"* Distribute the toy figures and say *Let's see if we can help solve this problem.*

Scaffolding Children's Learning
Encourage children to represent and act out the story with the figures and vehicles, and to use and create other props. If children play with the materials but do not act out a story, talk with them about the figures they use and their actions. Listen to, support, and comment on the ways children retell, change, or elaborate on the story. Talk about their ideas for solving the problem, and how and why they think it will work. Discuss their experiences with traffic jams and how people (e.g., parents) respond to them.

Vocabulary words: *busy, grown-up, halt, marching, parade, street, traffic jam*

Follow-up Ideas
Provide figures and props for children to re-enact familiar storybooks and nursery rhymes during other small-group times and work (choice) time. Encourage children to move like characters in stories at large-group time and during transitions. Carry props outside for children to re-enact scenes at outside time.

Where's the Rest?

What Children Do and Learn

Children listen to the middle of a familiar story, then draw and talk about what they think happens before and after the part they hear.

Content area:
Language, Literacy, and Communication

Time of day:
Small-group time

Materials
For each child and teacher: Paper, drawing and writing materials (e.g., crayons, markers, colored pencils)

To share: Copies of the middle pages of a storybook children are very familiar with, such as *Rosie's Walk* by Pat Hutchins

For backup: Figures and other small props that can be used to act out a story (e.g., small blocks, boxes, beads, shells, scarves)

Story Starter

Dexter and Cara went to a used book sale. That's where you can buy books that once belonged to other people who have finished reading them. Talk about the children's experiences buying books or other items at resale outlets. *Dexter and Cara picked out one of their favorite books,* Rosie's Walk, *and read the first page. The words said, "across the yard." The beginning of the book was missing! They turned to the last page and read, "over the haystack." The ending was missing too. No wonder no one wanted to read the book anymore!* Distribute the materials and say *I wonder if you can make up a beginning and an ending for the book.*

Scaffolding Children's Learning

As children work, ask what they think happened before and after the parts you read (e.g., *What do you think happened before Rosie walked across the yard? What do you suppose she did after going over the haystack?*) They may offer ideas from the actual book or make up their own stories. Encourage them to make a cover. If children use the materials to draw or write things unrelated to the story, talk about what they are making. Ask what they already drew and what they will draw next. Children may also choose to talk about their experiences with torn books, or how to take good care of books in the class library.

Children use figures and small props such as stones and shells to act out or represent the missing parts of a story.

Vocabulary words: *beginning, ending, first page, last page, missing, rest,*
sale, used

Follow-up Ideas

As you read storybooks with children, stop occasionally to ask what they
remember about what happened so far or what they think will happen
next. (Be careful not to interrupt the story too much or it will lose meaning and pleasure for the children.) Write a group story, with dictation,
where you supply the middle of the narrative and the children contribute
ideas for the beginning and the end. At large-group time, tell a story and
have children describe and act out what came before and what might
happen next.

Write Your Own Book 12

What Children Do and Learn
Children make books to explore the parts and order of printed materials.

Content area:
Language, Literacy, and Communication

Time of day:
Small-group time

Materials
For each child and teacher: Blank books (e.g., 8 1/2" x 17" sheets of paper folded in half)

To share: Crayons or markers; 3–4 books familiar to the children (for reference)

For backup: Extra blank books; sample real books

Story Starter
Donna was excited because she was going to the library. Talk about the children's experiences at the school or public library. *"Can you help me find a book on rainbows?" Donna asked the librarian. "I'm sorry," said the librarian. "They're all checked out. Do you want another book?" Donna was sad. She really wanted a book about rainbows. She decided to write one herself.* Take folded paper and markers, and say *She wrote the title and her name on the cover and drew a picture.* Ask the children for a title (such as *Rainbows*) and write it on the cover. Underneath write "by Donna" and draw a picture. *"Now I will draw more pictures and write my story," said Donna.* Open to the first page and talk about what Donna might write and draw in her book. Give the children their own blank books and say *I wonder what your books will be about.*

Scaffolding Children's Learning
Ask children what books they like, and encourage them to make their own books. They may write about rainbows or other topics, or just scribble or draw on the paper. Whatever they do, converse about their choice of materials and their actions making the "pages in their books." Refer to parts of a book, such as the title, author, print, illustration, first and last page, story (plot), and character. Use the sample books to point out typical book features and recall how book are read (front to back, top to bottom, left to right). Encourage children to tell you about their books and to share ("read") them with one another.

Vocabulary words: *author, character, checked out, illustration, library, page, title*

Follow-up Ideas
Add the children's books to the class library, and encourage children to "read" them silently or aloud. Children may want to take them home to read to their families. At large-group time, collaborate on a "class book" (e.g., about a field trip or other shared experiences). As you read books and other printed materials (magazines, catalogs, brochures, and so on) with children, point out various parts and call attention to how print is read.

6
Mathematics

The Mathematics story starters will help young children learn about these five important early math topics:

- *Number sense and operations* — Identifying numbers, counting things, and comparing amounts

- *Geometry* — Identifying shapes and understanding spatial relationships (position, distance, direction)

- *Measurement* — Using measurement tools, understanding units, and comparing measurements

- *Algebra* — Identifying and creating repeating patterns and increasing and decreasing patterns

- *Data analysis* — Collecting and charting information, using data to answer questions

13 Angela the Architect

Content area:
Mathematics

Time of day:
Small-group time

Materials

For each child and teacher: Disposable and recyclable construction materials (e.g., wood scraps, dowels, corks, Popsicle sticks, small cardboard boxes, empty plastic containers and lids); sturdy base for building on (e.g., heavy cardboard, plywood, plexiglass)

To share: Simple diagrams or "blueprints" of buildings (e.g., 1–2 stories tall, with 2–4 rooms, and doors and windows in different locations); make 3–4 different types of plans and photocopy several of each so children can choose among them

For backup: Glue, staplers, twine (if children want to attach and save their constructions); paper and writing tools if children want to draw their own blueprints; building designs in magazines or newspapers

What Children Do and Learn
Children build structures based on simple diagrams.

Story Starter

Angela was an architect. Her job was to draw blueprints, which are a kind of picture that helps construction workers know how to build things. Talk about buildings the children have seen under construction and how workers use blueprints to know how tall a building should be, where to put the doors, and so on. *Angela drew plans for houses, schools, and other places, so construction workers could build them.* With the children, look at a blueprint and say, for example, *Here's a two-story house with four rooms* or *This school has two classrooms and a gym.* Build all or part of a simple structure, inviting children's comments on the drawing and how to build it. Distribute the materials, indicate the blueprints, and say *I wonder what you will build.*

In talking to children about the structures they build, teachers can scaffold learning by encouraging the use of position, distance, and direction words.

Scaffolding Children's Learning

Talk with children about the plans and what they represent. Encourage the use of position, distance, and direction words, (e.g. *The bathroom is next to the bedroom; The offices are on the top floor and the restaurant is on the bottom floor*). To acknowledge children who build without referring to the plans, comment on their materials and actions. Compare the blueprints with the structures the children build. Describe, and encourage children to describe, what is the same and/or different. Support problem solving as children use the plans to guide their constructions. Encourage them to collaborate and help one another (e.g., *Cyrus, maybe Matt can show you how he got his water tower to balance on the roof*).

Vocabulary words: *architect, blueprint, building, construction, two-story*

Follow-up Ideas

Use blueprints (simple maps) of the classroom at planning and recall time. Encourage children to draw their own plans of the interest areas and/or storage units they use at work (choice) time. Put blueprints and writing materials in the art area for children who want to draw and/or construct their own plans. Encourage children to draw plans of the things they build in the block area. Look for blueprints and models or photos of finished buildings in architectural magazines or newspaper home improvement sections.

14 Dickering Dinosaurs

Content area:
Mathematics

Time of day:
Small-group time

Materials
For each child and teacher: Three blocks of different but similar lengths; ruler; strings of different lengths (longer, shorter, and same lengths as blocks)

To share: Other conventional and unconventional measuring tools (e.g., tape measure, strips of paper, rolls of receipt tape, Cuisenaire rods); blocks in other lengths

For backup: Paper and writing tools

What Children Do and Learn
Children use conventional and unconventional measuring tools to help "dinosaurs" (represented by blocks of different sizes) settle an argument about which one is the tallest.

Story Starter
Three dinosaurs disagreed about who was tallest. "I'm the tallest," said the Stegosaurus. "I'm taller than either of you," argued the Velociraptor. "You're both wrong," insisted the Triceratops, "I'm the tallest dinosaur of all!" "Tsk, tsk," said a wise little cockroach. There's a better way than dickering to figure out who's tallest." How else can they solve this problem? Solicit children's ideas, and say *The cockroach said they could* measure *to see who was tallest.* Give out the materials and say *I wonder who is the tallest, the shortest, and who's in the middle! Can you help the dinosaurs solve their problem?*

Children use math skills to resolve conflicts about size, distance, or other measurable properties.

Scaffolding Children's Learning

Talk with the children about their strategies for comparing the lengths of the blocks. If they say they can tell by looking, ask how they can be sure. For children who do not yet measure, help them line up the blocks next to one another and ask whether one is longer, shorter, or the same as another. Model correct measuring techniques, that is, begin measuring at the bottom (baseline) and start another unit at the point where the previous unit ended (without gaps or overlaps). Encourage children who are interested to trace the blocks on paper, then measure and compare the images. Young children are often fascinated by dinosaurs and know a great deal about them. Encourage children to share their knowledge with the group.

Vocabulary words: *cockroach, dickering, dinosaur, disagree, measure, tsk, wise*

Follow-up Ideas

Measure and record each child's height on a chart. Re-measure periodically and comment on how many inches taller they have grown. If children ask for your ideas to resolve conflicts related to length (e.g., who threw a beanbag farther; which train is the longest), suggest measuring when appropriate. Ask children how they will measure (e.g., what tools they will use, the unit of measurement, where they will begin and end measuring) and how they will use the results to solve the problem. Ask children to estimate the relative height or width of similar-size classroom objects and measure to verify their estimates.

15 Follow My Path

Content area:
Mathematics

Time of day:
Small-group time

Materials
For each child and teacher: Two kinds of small objects, at least six of each (e.g., stones, shells, acorns, beads, poker chips, wood chips, paper clips, squares of paper)

To share: Additional small objects

For backup: Paper or cardboard, and glue or tape (if children want to attach their paths)

What Children Do and Learn
Children make simple alternating patterns with small objects to represent paths in the woods.

Story Starter
Brenda and Darren liked to walk in the woods. Each path went to a special place — a pond, a meadow, and an old oak tree. Brenda said to Darren, "Let's take a walk. Maybe we'll discover a path to a place we've never been." But Darren had to clean his room, so they decided Brenda would start out and Darren would catch up when he finished. "How will I know which path to take?" he said. Ask for children's ideas. *Brenda said, "I'll mark my path with a shell, stone, shell, stone, shell, stone. Then you can follow my pattern into the woods."* Make this path, distribute materials, and say *I wonder what patterns you will make.*

Scaffolding Children's Learning
Describe and copy children's patterns (e.g., *Your path is a pattern that goes* acorn, bead, acorn, bead, acorn, bead). Start a path and ask children how to continue it (e.g., *Tell me what comes after the acorn*). Make a mistake and ask the children to help correct it (e.g., *Something doesn't look right. How can I fix it?*). For children who do not yet make patterns, say the order of their objects aloud but do not call it a pattern. Make patterns and non-patterns and ask children to guess what each one is. Encourage children who are ready to make complex patterns with two elements (AABAABAAB) or three elements (ABCABCABC).

Vocabulary words: *discover, follow, meadow, path, pattern, pond*

Follow-up Ideas
Use patterns during other parts of the daily routine (e.g., write the children's names on a chore list in alternating colors). Create, and encourage children to create, two-part movement sequences during large-group time; say the patterns aloud as you do them (e.g., pat and say, *Head, shoulders, head, shoulders, head, shoulders;* do at least three repeats). Point out visual patterns in children's clothes and room furnishings.

Mismatched Story Time

What Children Do and Learn

Children match counting bears and blocks in one-to-one correspondence, exploring concepts such as *too few, too many,* and *same number.*

Story Starter

Ms. Mismatch told the bears in her group to gather around for story time. She put out one chair, and all the bears tried to sit in it. Pile four bears on one block so they all tumble off. *"Oops," said Ms. Mismatch, "There aren't enough chairs for everyone to sit on."* She set out more chairs. Put out eight blocks and spread the four counting bears among them, leaving empty ones. *"That's not much better," sighed Ms. Mismatch. "Now there are too many chairs. The bears are so spread out they can't see the book or hear me read it. How can I match the number of chairs to the number of bears?"* Distribute the materials and say *Can you help poor Ms. Mismatch figure out how many chairs she needs so each bear has a place to sit and listen to the story?*

Content area:
Mathematics

Time of day:
Small-group time

Materials
For each child and teacher: 3–5 counting bears (or other small figures); 6–8 small (1"–2") blocks to serve as chairs

To share: Extra counting bears and blocks

For backup: None

In a variation of this activity, these children explore the concept of one-to-one correspondence using blocks and toy salamanders in a pretend "jungle" scenario.

Scaffolding Children's Learning

Talk about how children match the number of chairs and bears. Help them count (e.g., say a number as you put a bear on each block). For children who do not yet count, use general comparison words (e.g., *more* bears, *fewer* chairs than bears, the *same number* of chairs and bears). For those who are beginning to count, make numerical comparisons (e.g., *two fewer* bears than chairs). Pose simple challenges (e.g., *Suppose one more child joined Ms. Mismatch's group. How many chairs would she need so each child had a place to sit?; What if one child had to leave school early, right in the middle of story time?*).

Vocabulary words: *enough, everyone, extra, match, mismatch, number, spread out*

Follow-up Ideas

Encourage children to set the table at snacktime and mealtime, matching the number of place settings to the number of people. Ask how many fewer settings they need if there are absentees (e.g., *Jenny and Stuart are not here today. How many extra spoons are on the table?*) or how many more they need for visitors (e.g., *Ms. Valerie is joining us today. How many napkins should we add?*). When distributing materials at small- and large-group time, ask the children how many you need to give out so each child in the group has his or her own set. Provide objects for children to create matched sets in all areas of the room (e.g., nuts and bolts in the woodworking area, pegs and pegboards in the toy area, containers and lids in the house area).

Mixed-Up Treasure Maps 17

What Children Do and Learn
Children use a map of the classroom to find treasures hidden in areas where they don't belong.

Story Starter
(In a pirate's voice) *"Yo ho ho,"* said Captain Scrunch. *"I snuck into _____ (name of your school) last night and hid mixed-up treasures all around the room."* What do you think mixed-up treasures are? Talk to the children about their ideas. Then say *"My pirate mates and I hid things in parts of the room where they don't belong. But it was all in fun. We didn't want to confuse everyone for too long, so we left you maps showing where we hid things."* Distribute the maps and help the children identify familiar landmarks in the room. Say *Let's see if we can find the mixed-up treasures that Captain Scrunch hid around the room.*

Scaffolding Children's Learning
Help children use the maps, but expect that some will search for treasures without referring to the maps. Continue to point out landmarks and help children "rotate" the maps to orient themselves. Use, and encourage children to use, words related to position, direction, and distance (e.g., *It looks like the X is under the book area sign*). When children find a hidden treasure, help them connect the spot on the map to the location in the room. Encourage them to guess what is in the wrapped treasures based on their size and shape (or texture and sound if detectable) before they unwrap them. At the end of the activity, have children return the objects to their proper storage place, and point to the place on the map where they belong.

Vocabulary words: confuse, hid, map, mixed-up, scrunch, treasure

Follow-up Ideas
For a large-group time held outdoors, wrap and hide objects, and have children find them using a map of the outside play space. Provide wrapping materials and maps for children who want to hide and find objects at work (choice) time. At the beginning of cleanup time, have children mark on a map one or two objects that need to be returned to a different area of the classroom (e.g., blocks that were used to build a bed in the house area need to be returned to the block area). At message board time, use a map to mark where objects new to the classroom are wrapped and hidden. Encourage children to guess what and where they are.

Content area:
Mathematics

Time of day:
Small-group time or large-group time

Materials
For each child and teacher: Map of the classroom with X's marked where different treasures are hidden; include a few distinctive landmarks (e.g., sink, doors, windows, cubbies, bookshelves) and area signs and/or labels to help children orient and relate the map to the room

To share: Hidden treasures, wrapped and placed in locations where those objects would not ordinarily be (e.g., a block in the art area; a book under the blocks; a puzzle behind the message board)

For backup: Extra objects to hide when children are busy looking elsewhere (e.g., for children who have not found any or if all the objects are found before children lose interest in the search)

18 Monster Bed

Content area:
Mathematics

Time of day:
Small-group time

Materials
For each child and teacher: None

To share: Empty box tops or other flat rectangular containers ranging in size from 2"–3" to 24" per side; blocks of various sizes including some that are shorter and longer than the boxes; unconventional measuring tools (e.g., lengths of string or yarn; strips of paper in various lengths); and conventional measuring tools (e.g., rulers, tape measures)

For backup: None

What Children Do and Learn
Children explore conventional and unconventional measuring tools to see whether blocks of different sizes will fit inside a box.

Story Starter
Garabonga was growing up to be a humongous monster. How big do you think the monster was? Encourage children to describe or use their hands to show his size. *On his fifth birthday, his parents said, "You need a bigger bed* (point to the blocks), *but we have to choose one that fits inside your bedroom"* (point to the box tops). *Garabonga's bedroom was upstairs in the attic and the beds were heavy. His parents didn't want to carry each bed upstairs to see if it fit. So they measured his room and the beds first.* Model using a length of string to measure a box top (room) and a block (bed) to see if the bed fits. Try out the children's ideas. Ask each child to choose a box top and say *I wonder how you'll choose beds for these other bedrooms.*

Scaffolding Children's Learning
Talk with the children about their measurement strategies, including the tools they use, how they measure (e.g., where they begin and end, what to do if a side is longer or shorter than the tool), and how they use the results of their measuring to choose a bed or block. For children who do not yet measure, talk about their strategies for finding blocks that fit (e.g., trial and error, holding a block alongside the box, turning the box or block the shorter and/or longer way). Encourage children to measure and compare different sizes of boxes and blocks, and to try different measuring tools. Help them name the tools and describe what they observe as they use them, for example, whether something fits, overlaps, or extends beyond an edge.

As children work on building projects, encourage them to make measurement predictions and then to verify their estimates.

Vocabulary words: *attic, humongous, length, measure, ruler, width*

Follow-up Ideas

Store the materials in the block area for children to use at work (choice) time. Invite families to bring in unused box tops and other empty containers. Ask children what other tools, both conventional and unconventional, they can use for measuring. When children work on construction projects (e.g., with blocks or art materials), encourage them to measure beforehand to predict what will (or will not) fit, and then to verify their predictions. Encourage them to use different tools to measure things outdoors (e.g., how far they jump, the height of a ladder and the distance between its rungs, the distance between rows in the garden).

19 Number Fairies

Content area:
Mathematics

Time of day:
Large-group time

Materials
For each child and teacher:
Set of numerals 1–9 written on cardboard (approximately 3"–4" square) or small index cards (3" x 5") [Note: For younger children, or when it's early in the year, use numerals 1–3 or 1–5.]

To share: None

For backup:
Clipboard and marker (to tally how many of each numeral the class finds)

What Children Do and Learn
Children go on a walk in the neighborhood to find numbers and "number fairies" who grant them that number of wishes.

Story Starter
Today is Number Fairy Day, when the numbers turn into fairies and grant wishes. It works like this. When you see a number and say it out loud, the fairy lets you make that number of wishes. If you see the numeral 2 and say the word two, *then the Number 2 Fairy grants you two wishes.* Hold up a *2* and say the word *two. What two wishes would you make?* Solicit children's ideas. *What if I saw this number?* Hold up a *3.* Encourage children to say what the numeral is, and ask them what three wishes they would make. *We're going to walk around the neighborhood and see how many Number Fairies we can find. You can make your wishes in secret or you can share them with the rest of us.* Give each child a set of numerals and head out on your walk.

To build on this activity, provide numerals made of different materials, such as wood, felt, and foam, for children to manipulate.

Scaffolding Children's Learning
Help children find and name numerals. Invite them to make a corresponding number of wishes. Some may only want to find or match numerals, not make wishes. If children recognize that something is a numeral but do not know how to identify it, supply its name, or encourage children to ask one another for help (e.g., *Martina just saw the same number. Ask her how many wishes she made*). Help children keep track of the number of wishes by counting on your fingers or theirs, or by making tally marks. If children are interested, use the clipboard to keep track of how many of each numeral the class finds. Make comments such as *I wonder if you'll find a higher number next* or *That's a lower number than the last one we found.*

Vocabulary words: *grant, higher number, in secret, lower number, numeral*

Follow-up Ideas

Give children art materials to draw or paint their wishes. Talk about the number of wishes in their picture and encourage them to write the corresponding numeral on the paper. Provide numerals for them to trace or copy and, if children ask, write numerals for them. Look for numerals in the classroom and around the school building and play yard. Post numerals at the children's eye level and provide numerals (e.g., wooden, foam) throughout the room for them to hold, trace, and copy. Write numerals on the message board (e.g., draw two stick figures and write *2* to represent two visitors). Include books with large numerals in the class library.

20 Rescue the Kitty

Content area:
Mathematics

Time of day:
Small-group time

Materials
For each child and teacher: Set of 5 or more rectangular blocks or small boxes in different sizes

To share: Extra blocks and boxes

For backup: Small animal and people figures; paper and crayons and/or markers if children want to draw or trace their towers

What Children Do and Learn
Children explore rectangular blocks and boxes of different sizes as they construct a "ladder" to rescue a kitty stuck in a tree.

Story Starter
A kitty was stuck in a tree. Firefighters came to get the kitty down, but they forgot to bring their ladder! They saw a bunch of boxes of different sizes and decided to build a tower they could climb to rescue the kitty. Stack three blocks, putting a small one on the bottom or in the middle so that the tower falls. *"Something is not working,"* said one of the firefighters. *"The tower collapsed. What can we do so the tower won't fall down?"* Encourage children to contribute ideas, and try out their suggestions. Give each child a set of blocks and say *Let's see if you can find a way to rescue the kitty stranded up in the tree.*

Scaffolding Children's Learning
Encourage children to talk about the sizes of blocks they use and how they arrange them, using position words (e.g., *above, on top, underneath,* in the *middle*). Talk about how the size and arrangement of the blocks affect

Have small figures on hand to accompany children's block building as they act out and elaborate on the story.

their balance and the height of the towers children can build. Children may also elaborate on the story starter and/or make up their own stories to accompany their block building. If children use the blocks other than to build towers, talk with them about the sizes and arrangement of their blocks using position, distance, and direction words (e.g., *You put the biggest box in the* middle; *There's a square block on the* end *of each row; I wonder what you will do with the* upright *block*).

Vocabulary words: *big, bigger, biggest; collapse; rescue; top, middle, bottom; upright*

Follow-up Ideas
Provide blocks and boxes of many sizes for children to use at work (choice) time. Talk to them about the materials and actions they use, and the position of objects, as they construct things. Take pictures of children's constructions at various stages and encourage children to sequence and describe them.

21 Robot Trail Mix

Content area:
Mathematics

Time of day:
Small-group time

Materials
For each child and teacher: 6–8 of each "robot trail mix" ingredient (e.g., small animals, beads, shells, pegs, nuts and bolts, buttons, golf tees); bowl and spoon

To share: Charts listing the ingredients (in pictures and words) in one column with tally marks (e.g., checks or slashes) and numerals next to them in the second column indicating preferences for each; 2–3 copies of several different charts (e.g., one chart indicating 3 beads, 5 shells, and 2 pegs; another chart indicating 2 counting bears, 1 peg, and 4 buttons; and so on)

For backup: Blank charts with two columns; writing tools

What Children Do and Learn
Children decide the composition of "robot trail mix" based on charts indicating the robots' preferences for each "ingredient."

Story Starter
Mr. Droid owned a store where robots shopped for food. What do you think robots like to eat? Discuss the children's ideas. *Their favorite food was Robot Trail Mix, which has beads, screws, and other crunchy things in it. But Mr. Droid didn't know how much of each ingredient to put in the trail mix, so he asked the robots to check the ones they liked best on a chart.* Share and discuss a chart with the children; for example, you might say, *They liked shells most because it has five checks, pegs least because it has only two checks, and beads in the middle with three checks.* Count out the ingredients together and stir them in a bowl. Ask them to choose a chart, distribute the other materials, and say *I wonder how much of each ingredient you'll put in your trail mix.*

Scaffolding Children's Learning
For children who do not use the charts or count, talk about their actions in comparison terms (e.g., *none, many, few, a lot, a little, more, less, the same*). Help those who use the charts to count ingredients. Model counting strategies (e.g., touch each object as it is counted). Connect the data on the charts to children's actions, e.g., *You put four beads in the bowl, like the number 4 next to that picture.* Do not correct errors, but say something like *You put in one extra golf tee. Do your robots like golf tees?* Encourage those who are interested to make their own charts, and (if asked), help them write labels and numerals.

Vocabulary words: *count, crunchy, extra, favorite, ingredient, least, most*

Follow-up Ideas
Chart the children's preferences and use the data to make trail mix at snacktime. Discuss which ingredients children like the most, the least, and a middle amount. Solicit their ideas on what to do if there are no check marks next to an ingredient (i.e., introduce the concept of *zero*). Encourage children to chart the number of items they use in their play activities (e.g., the number of each size block in a tower or each art material in a collage). Keep track of which songs are requested at large-group time to identify class favorites.

Shape Tales

What Children Do and Learn
Children use paper shapes (triangles, circles, and rectangles) in different sizes and colors to create and tell stories.

Content area:
Mathematics

Time of day:
Small-group time

Materials
For each child and teacher: Paper circles, triangles, and rectangles (including squares), each in 2–3 sizes and in different colors (a total of 10–15 shapes per person); sheet of white paper on which to place the shapes

To share: Extra sheets of paper; other shapes, such as diamonds, stars, hexagons, ovals, parallelograms

For backup: Tape and glue for children to attach the shapes to the paper; writing tools to label the pictures

Story Starter
One day, an elephant rowed his boat across the lake. Place a long rectangle (boat) on a sheet of paper and put a large circle (elephant) on top of it. *The sun was very hot, so the elephant put a hat on top of his head. What shape should I use for a hat?* Place the suggested shape (e.g., a medium-size triangle) above the large circle. *He put his trunk in the water and blew bubbles.* Line up three small circles coming out of the big circle. *A bird flew down and popped the bubbles with its beak.* Touch the point of a small triangle to each small circle and make popping sounds with the children. *Then the elephant rowed back home.* Slide the rectangle across the page and move the big circle to a big square (or whatever shape children choose for a house). Distribute the shapes and sheets of paper and say *I wonder what stories you will tell with your shapes.*

Scaffolding Children's Learning
Talk about the shapes the children use to create their stories. They may retell your story, invent their own stories, or just play with the shapes without telling stories. Name and encourage children to name shapes and compare their sizes. Discuss the position of the shapes on the page and in relation to one another (e.g., *You put three circle pizzas in a row on the bottom of the page, with a pepperoni square on top of each one*). Talk about what makes a shape a shape (e.g., number of angles and sides; curved and straight edges), regardless of size or color. Use words for position (e.g., *above, below, opposite*), direction (e.g., *across, up, down*), and distance (e.g., *near, far, close to*). Encourage children to detail their story ideas and write or dictate them to you.

Vocabulary words: *angle, beak, circle, curved, rectangle, straight, triangle*

Follow-up Ideas
Display children's stories or make them into a book. If children want to continue working on their shape tales at work (choice) time, put them in a safe place with a work-in-progress sign. Put leftover and additional shape cutouts in the art area. Encourage children to make regular and irregular shapes to add to the collection. Make a felt or flannel board with shapes in a variety of sizes and colors for children to create their own stories, or to represent the stories in familiar books, fairy tales, songs, and other narratives.

23 Snow People Patterns

Content area:
Mathematics

Time of day:
Small-group time

Materials
For each child and teacher: 5–10 small circles each of red, blue, and yellow paper

To share: Extra circles in different colors; paper cut into other shapes

For backup: Paper and glue or tape (if children want to attach and save their snow people); crayons and markers to decorate snow people

What Children Do and Learn
Children make snow people with paper shapes, creating simple alternating patterns of two or three colors, and changing patterns by adding or taking away shapes.

Story Starter
Have you ever been to the Land of Colored Snow? Ask what the children think it looks like. *Instead of the snow being white, it comes in red, blue, and yellow. The snow people who live there come in colors too. Some are red and yellow.* Make a snow person alternating red and yellow circles (red, yellow; red, yellow; red, yellow; with at least three repeats). *Other snow people are yellow and blue* (make a snow person with three yellow-blue repeats). *Whenever a snow family has a new baby, they wonder what colors will be in its pattern.* Distribute the materials. Say *I wonder what patterns your snow babies and snow people will have.*

Scaffolding Children's Learning
Recite children's patterns aloud, and encourage them to do the same. For those who do not yet make patterns, name the order of their colors but do not call it a pattern. Copy children's patterns and ask what you'll need to make one like theirs. Start a pattern and ask children to help you continue it. Leave a blank space for them to fill in. Make a mistake to see if they correct you. If not, say *Something is wrong. How can I fix it?* Pose challenges (e.g., *Suppose all the blue snow melted. How could you change your pattern?*). For children who are ready, extend the story. *Really tall snow people have two of each color* (make an AABBAABBAABB pattern, e.g., red, red, yellow, yellow, etc., with three repeats). *There's even a snow king and queen who add one more of each color the taller they get!* Make a snow person with one yellow, two blue, and three red circles. Ask for help making a snow person that "adds" or "takes away" a circle with each extension.

Vocabulary words: *extend, lengthen, pattern, primary color, shorten*

Follow-up Ideas
Add colored circles to the art area. Repeat this activity using paper cut in different shapes (e.g., tell a story about the land of "shape rain" in which the rivers run in shape patterns). Look for patterns of alternating colors or shapes in the classroom. At cleanup time, challenge children to stack blocks, toy figures, and similar materials in patterns on the shelf. Go on a pattern hunt and search for patterns in nature (e.g., variegated leaves and caterpillars) and in the neighborhood (e.g., window curtains).

Wacky Play Time

What Children Do and Learn
Children combine and divide a set of ten objects into four groups of varying numbers.

Story Starter
Today is Wacky Play Time. Ask what the children think *wacky* means. *At Wacky Play Time, silly things happen in each area of the room. In the toy area, the puzzle pieces don't fit together. In the book area, the pages are glued together. What wacky thing do you think happens in the house (art) area?* Solicit children's ideas. *Ten animals went to different areas for Wacky Play Time. Two did wacky puzzles, four read wacky books, one did ___ and three did ___* (use the children's idea for the house and art areas). *Some animals changed areas and some stayed in the same area the whole playtime.* Switch some animals and leave others in place. Distribute the materials, and say *I wonder which wacky areas your animals will play in.*

Scaffolding Children's Learning
Some children may talk about what happens in the wacky areas, others will choose to just move animals around on the paper. Talk about how many animals play in each area and help children count them. For children who do not yet count, talk about which area has *more, fewer,* or the *same* number of animals. If they switch animals to different area(s), ask how many that leaves or adds to each area. Comment on how children add to, subtract from, or divide the number of animals in their groups. For children who are ready, use simple fractions (e.g., *Half your animals are doing wacky puzzles*). Introduce the idea of *none* or *zero*. Encourage interested children to divide pieces of paper into more or fewer areas.

Vocabulary words: *add to, combine, divide, fraction, subtract from, wacky*

Follow-up Ideas
At planning and recall time, talk about how many children in the group will (or did) play in each area. Keep a chart of how many children use each area over the course of a week. Talk about how the same number of children can be divided in different ways (i.e., distribute themselves among the interest areas). When there are choices at snacktime or mealtime, comment on how many children choose each option (e.g., *Of the six children in our group, three ate apple slices, two ate pear slices, and one ate some of each*). Encourage children to describe and count the number of children according to other category divisions (e.g., *Seven have brown hair, two are blonde, and one is a redhead*).

Content area:
Mathematics

Time of day:
Small-group time

Materials
For each child and teacher: 10 small animal figures (they do not all have to be the same as long as each child has 10 of them); 1 piece of paper divided into four sections with a familiar area sign or symbol in each [Note: For younger children, start with five figures and two areas.]

To share: Extra animals; blank paper and writing tools

For backup: Drawing materials

7
Science and Technology

The story starters in Science and Technology encourage children to observe, make predictions, experiment, gather information, and draw conclusions about

- *Collections* — Describing and sorting things based on one or more attributes and using all the senses

- *Environment* — Investigating the natural world (plants, animals, weather, bodies) and how we take care of it

- *Operations and functions* — Seeing how things work including cause-and-effect relationships, time, speed, and sequence

- *Technology* — Discovering and following procedures for operating simple equipment

25 Big Teeny

Content area:
Science and Technology

Time of day:
Small-group time

Materials
For each child and teacher: Magnifying glass; sheet of white paper to use as a backdrop

To share: Variety of objects with interesting marks and textures not easily visible to the naked eye (e.g., shells, feathers, dyed onion skin, tread marks on wheeled toys, newsprint, crayon marks and brush strokes on paper, walnut shells, woven and knitted fabrics, wood grain, dried plants, and insects)

For backup: Other magnifying tools (e.g., old eyeglasses, binoculars, telescope, microscope)

What Children Do and Learn
Children explore a variety of objects with magnifying glasses to observe details they cannot see with the naked eye.

Story Starter
Far, far away from where we live is the make-believe planet of Big Teeny. Since big *is another word for* large (hold your hands far apart and open your eyes wide) *and* teeny *means really* small (hold your thumb and forefinger close together and squint your eyes), *why do you suppose the planet is named* Big Teeny? Solicit the children's ideas. Talk about things that are very big and very small. *On planet Big Teeny, all the people can see the big things but they have to use magnifying glasses to see the really small things.* Distribute the materials, and say *I wonder what we'll see looking through our magnifying glasses.*

Children explore objects with a variety of interesting marks and textures not visible to the naked eye by using a magnifying glass.

Scaffolding Children's Learning

Encourage children to examine objects first with their naked eye and then with the magnifying glass. Ask what looks the same and what looks different. Talk about the details they see when something is magnified. Children may also enjoy looking at themselves, at you, and at one another through the lens (e.g., at fingernails, strands of hair, noses, and clothing). Encourage children to experiment and observe the magnified effects (e.g., writing with different color or width crayons to see whether the detailed view changes; soaking objects in water and observing changes in size, color, and structure).

Vocabulary words: *binoculars, enlarge, eyeglasses, magnified, microscope, telescope*

Follow-up Ideas

With the children, choose an area of the classroom to put the magnifying glasses. Use them outside to look at insects, plants, stones, siding, pavement, and other objects and surfaces. Encourage children to draw and compare the details of things seen with their naked eye versus under a magnifying glass. Provide other things that magnify or reduce images (e.g., eyeglasses [families may donate old pairs], cameras, binoculars, telescopes). Enlarge and shrink images and fonts on computer screens and discuss these effects.

26 Falling Down

Content area:
Science and Technology

Time of day:
Large-group time

Materials
For each child and teacher: Paper bags or other containers that are easy to carry

To share: None

For backup: None

What Children Do and Learn
Children go on a neighborhood walk to observe the seasonal changes taking place in their environment as summer turns to fall.

Story Starter
One hot summer day, Sally rode her bike and swam in the lake. "I'm tired," she yawned, and fell asleep for a long time in the hammock. When she woke up, everything was different. The leaves weren't green any more. They were yellow, orange, and red. Many had fallen to the ground. "What happened?" she asked Bart the Bird. "Summer's over. It's a different season. It's fall," he chirped. "Come look." Bart flew slowly, and Sally walked beside him. Give each child a paper bag, and say *Let's fly out the door and walk slowly too. I wonder what things we'll see. We can collect them and bring them back to the classroom.*

Encourage children to use different senses to describe how fall looks, feels, sounds, and smells.

Scaffolding Children's Learning

Talk about how children move out the door, including the type and speed of their motions. Encourage them to collect things such as leaves and dried grasses from the ground; caution them not to take anything still attached to a living plant. Talk about the properties of the objects the children observe and collect, and other characteristics of the outdoors (e.g., the quality of the light, temperature, wind). Encourage them to use all their senses to describe how things look and smell, feel different textures, and listen to the sounds of rustling leaves or scampering squirrels. Ask what else the sensations remind them of.

Vocabulary words: *chirped, fall, hammock, rustle, season, summer, yawned*

Follow-up Ideas

At small-group time, encourage children to sort and describe the things they collected on the walk. Provide materials, such as paper and glue, children can use if they choose to make a collage. Add the materials children have collected to the art area or toy area. Go on neighborhood walks to observe other seasonal changes (see activity #33, "Springing Up"). Encourage children to describe what they observe at outside time, using all their senses. Bring in artwork reproductions, magazine photos, and other images that depict the change in seasons. Talk about how the clothing the children are wearing changes with the season and why they think this is so.

27 Fruit Finds

Content area:
Science and Technology

Time of day:
Small-group time (can combine with snacktime or mealtime)

Materials
For each child and teacher: 2 whole fruits (need not be the same 2 for each person; have at least 6 types for variety); safety knives; small cutting board (plastic or wood); paper plates or absorbent towels; one small paper cup

To share: Additional whole fruits; fruits that are hard to cut may be pre-sliced or cut in half to start; large bowl(s) to hold cut-up fruit for fruit salad

For backup: Extra small paper cups; chart paper and markers

Note: Have children wash their hands or use hand wipes at the beginning of the activity; cut-up fruit can be made into a fruit salad and shared at snacktime or mealtime.

What Children Do and Learn
Children cut up various fruits, then make and eat a fruit salad, as they observe, describe, and compare the fruits using all their senses (sight, smell, taste, sound, and touch).

Story Starter
Willie the Worm crawled into the fruit bowl. "Inch" your forefinger along the table. *"Which fruit should I eat first?" he asked.* Name the fruits with the children. *His sharp teeth bit into the soft skin of a round, red apple. He wondered what it was like* inside *the apple. Willie crawled in and what do you think he found?* Cut the apple, give each child a small piece, and discuss their observations. Put extra pieces in the large bowl. *Willie ate 'til he was so full, he fell asleep. He didn't try any other fruits. But our stomachs are bigger so we can try them all and make a fruit salad!* Distribute materials, and say, *I wonder what we'll discover about our fruits.* Remind children to use their own cup and only put untasted pieces in the large bowl to share later.

Children predict what the inside of an apple will look like, then cut it open to explore and describe its colors, seeds, texture, smell, and taste.

Scaffolding Children's Learning

Encourage children to use all their senses as they explore the fruit. Describe, and encourage children to describe, visual characteristics of the fruit (e.g., color, shape, size; presence of seeds or pits); sound (e.g., *Do you hear anything when you shake it? Is it squeaky or quiet when you bite it?*); texture (e.g., creamy, pulpy, tough, soft); smell (e.g., sweet, citrusy), and taste (e.g., bitter, tangy, spicy). Ask what the attributes remind them of (e.g., *Does it smell like something else? Is the texture like something you eat or play with?*) Encourage children to predict what a fruit will look or feel like inside and verify their predictions after they cut it open. Ask them to guess what it will taste like. Pose questions like *Why do you think some fruits have pits and some don't?* If children are interested, make a chart listing the characteristics of each fruit.

Vocabulary words: *drippy, ooze, pulpy, sour, sweet, tangy, tough*

Follow-up Ideas

Survey which fruits children like best and use the information to create a recipe for the next time the class has fruit salad. Encourage children to represent (e.g., draw or paint) the fruit whole and cut up. Repeat this activity with vegetables, grains, dips, or other foodstuffs. At snacktimes and mealtimes, encourage children to describe and compare what they are eating based on various sensory properties. Ask children about the foods their families eat at home, and encourage them to describe these foods in terms of appearance, sounds, textures, smells, and tastes.

28 Magnet Car

Content area:
Science and
Technology

Time of day:
Small-group time

Materials
*For each child and
teacher:* 1 magnet
(a size that the child
can easily hold
and maneuver),
4–6 magnetic
and nonmagnetic
objects (e.g.,
paper clips, metal
and plastic eating
utensils, nails,
screws, golf tees,
tools with metal
heads and wooden
or plastic handles
[screw driver,
hammer], all-metal
tools [wrench],
metal and plastic
buttons, wooden or
plastic beads, small
wooden blocks,
plastic animal
figures, plastic pens
with metal clip-ons,
zippers)

To share: Additional
magnetic and
nonmagnetic
objects

For backup: Blocks
to build a road;
chart paper and
markers

What Children Do and Learn
Children drive a "magnet car" to explore which objects are and are not
attracted to the magnet.

Story Starter
Spread three or four magnetic and nonmagnetic objects on the table,
and say *Mrs. Molloy drove her magnet car down the road.* Slide a magnet
between two objects. *She wanted to turn in this direction* (gesture with
your right hand), *but there was a paper clip on her other side* (gesture left)
so the magnet car veered that way and stuck (demonstrate with a metallic
object). *A police officer pulled them apart. Mrs. Molloy's magnet car drove
past a plastic bead* (demonstrate), *but when she passed a spoon it stuck to
her car. "Oh dear," she said, "To get where I'm going, I have to stay away
from things that stick to my magnet car!"* Distribute the materials, and say
*Let's help Mrs. Molloy figure out which things she shouldn't drive close to and
which ones she can get past.*

Scaffolding Children's Learning
As children explore, encourage them to label materials and describe what
is happening. For children mainly interested in "driving" the magnet, ask
their permission to put various "obstacles" in the way. Pose challenges
(e.g., *I wonder how close you can get with your car before the magnet pulls
the paper clip toward it*). Encourage children to make predictions, verify,
and explain their findings (e.g., *Why do you think it did [not] attach to the
magnet?*). If children are interested, help them draw and label a chart
listing magnetic and nonmagnetic objects. Discuss what the objects in
the two categories have in common and how they are different.

Vocabulary words: *attract, direction, magnetic, nonmagnetic, veered,
whoosh*

Follow-up Ideas
Put magnets and a variety of metal and nonmetal objects in the toy area
or at the sand table. At another small- or large-group time, give each child
a magnet and take a "magnet walk" around the room or building. Bring a
clipboard to keep track of what is (not) magnetic. Invite families to send
in collections (e.g., in small bags) of magnetic and nonmagnetic items for
children to explore and sort. Hide metallic and nonmetallic objects in a
bag, ask children to predict by feel whether they are magnetic, and then
verify their predictions by appearance and with a magnet.

Rain Boots

What Children Do and Learn
Children drip colored water on different surfaces to explore which ones do and do not absorb liquid.

Story Starter
One day it rained as hard as a shower turned on full blast! Everyone asked Sal the Shoemaker to make them rain boots so their feet wouldn't get wet. Sal made rubber boots and, when he ran out of rubber, he made boots out of paper, foil, and cardboard. Show children these materials. *People wore their boots in the rain. Some told Sal, "My feet stayed dry."* Put a drop of water on the boot and another nonabsorbent surface. Let children see the water run off and feel the inside or underside to confirm it is dry. *But others complained, saying "These paper boots are no good. Water seeped in and my feet got wet."* Drip water onto an absorbent surface, and let children observe and feel how the moisture spreads. *Sal had to figure out what to make the boots out of.* Distribute the materials and say *Let's help Sal. I wonder if the water will run off or soak into these things.*

Scaffolding Children's Learning
As children drip water on a variety of surfaces, discuss their observations. Ask *Does the water soak in? Does the color spread? Does the water bead up on the surface?* For children who are more interested in using the eyedropper than comparing surfaces, talk about what happens when they squeeze the dropper (e.g., *Where does the water go? What happens to it?*). Encourage children to add another color of water, and see whether or not the colors blend depending on the absorbency of the surface. Mix solutions of different thickness, and observe whether and how fast they are absorbed by different surfaces.

Vocabulary words: absorb, moisture, run off, soak in, spread, surface

Follow-up Ideas
Stock assorted papers and applicators in the art area. Provide different textiles at the water table and encourage children to experiment by dipping them in water and dripping water on them. Provide sponges of different sizes and densities for children to compare the volume and rate of absorption. After a rain shower, encourage children to note and compare where water is (not) absorbed (e.g., sand, mud, grass, pavement, oil-slicked areas). Pour buckets of water outside on different surfaces so children can predict where it will soak in, run, or bead up.

Content area:
Science and Technology

Time of day:
Small-group time

Materials
For each child and teacher: 3–4 absorbent and nonabsorbent surfaces (e.g., drawing paper, paper towel, coffee filter, sponge, ink blotter, grocery bag, foil, wax paper, Styrofoam tray, small rubber mat, manila folder, cardboard); plastic cup of tinted water (add a small amount of paint or food coloring); eyedropper

To share: Rubber boot; additional surfaces; other water-applicators (e.g., paintbrush, plastic spoons); cups, water, and paint or food coloring to mix other colors in thin and thick solutions

For backup: None

30 Roly-Poly

Content area:
Science and
Technology

Time of day:
Small-group time

Materials
*For each child and
teacher:* 4 objects
including some
that roll and some
that do not (e.g.,
different types of
balls [rubber ball,
tennis ball, Ping-
Pong ball], wheeled
toys, round and
rectangular
blocks, round and
rectangular beads,
acorns, pencils,
markers, pens
with clips [i.e., not
perfect cylinders],
empty spools,
chalk, marbles,
buttons, round
and S-shaped
packaging pellets,
beanbags, empty
paper towel rolls);
and a smooth and
sturdy surface to
roll objects on (e.g.,
wood or plastic
board, thick-coated
cardboard)

To share: Additional
objects for rolling;
different surfaces

For backup: Chart
paper with two
columns (i.e., to
draw or write which
objects do and
do not roll) and
markers

What Children Do and Learn
Children experiment with objects of different shapes and sizes to see what
does and does not roll.

Story Starter
*The people who live in Roly-Poly don't walk. They just roll. They don't run or
hop or skip or jump. All they do is ___ (pause for the children to say* roll*).
They don't slide, glide, leap, or pirouette. They just ___ (pause again for children to say* roll*). Whenever the people in Roly-Poly go somewhere, they roll
there. All the toys the children play with have to roll too — like balls. Also,
the food everyone eats has to roll — like peas.* Solicit the children's ideas
about other toys and foods that do or do not roll. Give each child four
objects and a flat surface, and say *I wonder which of these things will roll.*

Scaffolding Children's Learning
Encourage children to try a variety of objects and share their observations about which do (not) roll. Imitate their experiments (e.g., starting
from different positions, orienting objects in different ways). Ask them
to show or tell you what they did so you can get the same results. For
children who are interested in exploring rather than rolling objects, talk
about the characteristics of the items they play with (e.g., size, shape,
texture). Encourage children to predict what will (not) roll and to verify
their predictions. Ask why their predictions did (not) match what happened. Offer challenges (e.g., *Could you get it to roll if you held it a different
way?*) If children are interested, help them make a chart of objects that do
and do not roll.

Vocabulary words: *circular, flat, globe, pirouette, rectangular, roly-poly*

Follow-up Ideas
Make a Roly-Poly book for the class library in which children can add
drawings, words, and photographs of objects that do (not) roll (draw
a "do not" symbol [Ø] around those that don't roll). At outside time,
encourage children to predict and verify which items will (not) roll
and on which surfaces. Encourage children to try rolling their own bodies
in various ways. Imitate their actions. Set up two cartons in the classroom, one marked "O" and the other marked "Ø" and encourage families
to bring in used or recyclable objects that do and do not roll. When you
play guessing games with the children (e.g., *I'm thinking of something that
___. Can you guess what it is?*), include whether or not the object rolls as
one of the clues.

88   *Story Starters*

Shrinking and Swelling

31

What Children Do and Learn
Children explore how ice cubes and sponges get smaller (shrink) and bigger (swell), respectively, with the loss or absorption of water.

Story Starter
Ike the Ice Cube and Sonya the Sponge went out in a rowboat on a sweltering hot summer day. Put an ice cube and a piece of dry sponge on your tray. *As the heat from the sun beat down on them, Ike began to melt and he got smaller and smaller.* Roll your ice cube on the tray. *The water puddled on the bottom of the rowboat, where Sonya's feet were resting.* Place the sponge so it is resting in some of the melted area. *As the water rose up from the floor of the boat through Sonya's feet, what do you think happened to her?* Talk to the children about their ideas. Comment on how the sponge swells and gets bigger. Give each child an ice cube, a piece of dry sponge, and a tray. *Let's see what happens to Ike and Sonya as they continue to sit in the hot sun.* [Suggestion: With younger children, do shrinking (Ike) OR swelling (Sonya). With older children, use both.]

Scaffolding Children's Learning
Talk with the children about their observations. Encourage them to describe and explain what happens to the ice cube and to the sponge. For children who are ready, discuss contrasts in the ice cube versus the sponge, such as getting bigger and smaller, shrinking and swelling, becoming wetter or drier. Observe and describe the processes of transformation as things melt, change size, and add or lose water. Encourage children to predict what will happen and to verify their predictions. Pose questions such as, *Why do you think Ike got smaller? I wonder how Ike and Sonya could get to be the same size?*

Vocabulary words: absorb, damp, melt, shrink, sweltering, swell

Follow-up Ideas
Add the materials (make ice cubes the night before) to the water table. Bring ice cubes and sponges outside. Encourage children to see what happens when they put various materials in containers of water or puddles, or when they expose them to sunshine or shade. Comment on what happens to sponges and paper towels when children wet them at cleanup time. Trace dry sponges, wet them, and retrace them to compare their sizes. Do this process in reverse (trace a wet sponge and retrace it as it dries).

Content area:
Science and Technology

Time of day:
Small-group time

Materials
For each child and teacher: Ice cube, small rectangular piece of dry sponge (1/2" to 1" per side), tray

To share: Extra ice cubes and pieces of sponge

For backup: Other absorbent materials that swell when they get wet (e.g., cotton balls, swabs) and materials that do not swell when they get wet (e.g., fabric swatches)

32 Snail Trails

Content area:
Science and Technology

Time of day:
Small-group time

Materials
For each child and teacher: Paper, paintbrush, and a small cup of paint (use easily visible colors such red, blue, purple, or green; one color per person; they need not be the same color)

To share: "Resist" materials such as adhesive and masking tape, wax rubbed on paper (e.g., from candles, white crayons, beeswax), strips of plastic wrap or foil to tape on paper, shiny (plastic coated) stickers

For backup: Additional resist materials; nonresist materials (e.g., scraps of fabric, nonshiny stickers)

What Children Do and Learn
Children explore and explain why paint does not leave marks on areas of paper that have been treated with various "resist" materials such as masking tape.

Story Starter
Using a piece of paper with strips of tape in several places and a brush dipped in red paint, say *Once a snail was crawling along the road, leaving a trail of red behind him.* Stroke the brush across the paper, crossing a taped area where the paint will not stick. *But when he looked back, he saw a spot was missing.* Ask the children why they think this happened. Paint over the same spot (re-dip the brush in paint if needed) so the children can again see it remains bare. Rub wax on another part of the paper, and say *The snail continued on his way, but another bare area appeared.* Demonstrate, this time crossing the waxed area. *The snail was puzzled. He said, "I wonder why some spots have paint and some are bare."* Talk with children about their ideas. Distribute the materials and say *Let's see what happens when your snails cross the paper.*

Scaffolding Children's Learning
Encourage children to share their actions, observations, and explanations (*I wonder why it's blank here; What do you think would happen if…?*). If children are just interested in painting, support their efforts by imitating their movements and commenting on what they paint. Encourage children to paint on different materials and compare their effects. Help them distinguish (i.e., classify) areas that do and do not take the paint. Talk about contrasting characteristics, such as painted versus unpainted, colored versus uncolored, and dark versus light. Describe the position and direction of children's actions as they move their brushes across, up and down, and around the edges of the paper.

Vocabulary words: bare, missing, puzzled, resist, snail, trail

Follow-up Ideas
Provide various resist materials in the art area. When children paint or draw (e.g., across a collage they have created), encourage them to predict whether the brush or marker will (not) leave color. After a rain, observe how oily areas on the ground are not wet and encourage children to say why they think this is so. Encourage them to compare materials on their own clothes (e.g., rubber boots versus cloth sneakers, rain slickers versus cotton jackets) that do or do not absorb water, and to describe and classify what they see.

Springing Up

> ## What Children Do and Learn
> Children go on a neighborhood walk to observe the seasonal changes taking place in their environment as winter turns to spring.

Content area:
Science and Technology

Time of day:
Large-group time

Materials
For each child and teacher: Paper bags or other containers that are easy to carry

To share: None

For backup: None

Story Starter
One very cold day, a big brown bear ate two bags of apples, three peanut butter sandwiches, and four bowls of broccoli with garlic sauce. What else do you think he ate? Solicit children's ideas. *It started to snow, so he crawled inside a hollow log and fell asleep. He slept a long time. When he awoke and peeked outside, the snow was melted. Winter was over and spring, a new season, was here. Little green shoots poked out of the ground and from branches. "I'm ravenously hungry," said the bear. He crawled out of his log and lumbered off to see what he could find. Let's crawl to the door and lumber off to see what spring looks like here.*

Scaffolding Children's Learning
Talk about how the children move, for example, noting their body positions when they change from crawling to being upright. Ask what they think *lumber* means. Distribute paper bags for them to collect things, such as fallen twigs or blossoms. Caution against taking anything still alive and growing. Talk about the properties of the objects children observe and collect, as well as other features of the outdoors (e.g., the quality of the light, temperature, wind). Encourage them to use all their senses (i.e., to describe how things look and smell, to feel different textures, to listen to the sounds of chirping birds or fluttering breezes).

Vocabulary words: hollow, lumber (verb), peeked, ravenously, season, spring, winter

Follow-up Ideas
At small-group time, encourage children to sort and describe what they collected. Provide paper and fastening materials if children want to use them to make a collage. Add the collected materials to the art area or toy area. For another large-group time, retell the story about the bear and have children add to it and act it out, using things they collected as props. Go on neighborhood walks to observe other seasonal changes (see activity #26, "Falling Down"). Encourage children to describe what they observe at outside time, using all their senses.

34 Stick it to Me

Content area:
Science and Technology

Time of day:
Small-group time

Materials
For each child and teacher: 4–6 objects of different textures and weight, some that stick to the tape(s) and lift easily (e.g., pieces of paper, fabric, cotton balls) and some that do not (e.g., heavy metal bolts or blocks); scissors, if children want to cut rather than tear tape

To share: Rolls of different types of tape (magnetic tape, masking tape, duct tape, electrician's tape)

For backup: Additional materials on which to stick tape (e.g., Styrofoam pieces, wax paper, Ping-Pong and golf balls, clay, and play dough); chart paper and markers

What Children Do and Learn
Children explore different types of tape with materials of varying weight and texture to see how strongly each kind of tape sticks.

Story Starter
The tape rolls had a sticking contest to see which was the stickiest. Let's see what kinds of tape we have. With the children, feel the adhesives and name the types of tape. *The tape rolls wondered who could stick to the most things and who was strong enough to lift up the objects. "I can," said Magnetic Tape. "I bet I can," said Masking Tape.* Cut or tear a piece of each type of tape and try to lift a light-weight and a heavy-weight object. Talk about the children's observations. Repeat the comparison rolling each type of tape into a ball. Distribute the materials and say *I wonder how sticky each type of tape is. Will it be sticky enough to lift these things?*

Scaffolding Children's Learning
Encourage children to explore and describe which objects each type of tape sticks to and the things it is strong enough to lift. Some children will explore tearing, cutting, balling, or sticking the tape, without comparing the strength of the adhesive. Talk about children's actions and what they discover. Encourage those who try different combinations of tape and objects to describe and explain what they observe (e.g., *This [magnetic] tape can't lift the block but this [electrician's] tape can. I wonder why?*). Pose challenges (e.g., *I want to lift the bolt. Which tape do you think I should use?*). Encourage children to explore and compare using flat pieces and balls of tape. If they are interested, make a chart showing what things each type of tape can lift.

Vocabulary words: *adhesive, balling, cling, magnetic, masking, sticky, tape*

Follow-up Ideas
Stock a variety of tapes and other adhesives (e.g., glue, paste) in the art area. As children construct things, ask how they will attach the parts. Discuss their problem-solving strategies when the things they try do not work. Provide other materials to compare sticking properties, such as objects that are wet or dry, or smooth or textured. Explore other materials that stick together (e.g., Velcro, pieces of felt). Discuss things that naturally stick to children's clothes or hair (e.g., burrs or thistles, cobwebs), and invite children's explanations.

Toy Speedway

35

What Children Do and Learn
Children explore, predict, and verify the rate of movement of sliding and rolling various objects across different types of surfaces.

Story Starter
Ladies and gentlemen. Welcome to the ___ (insert the name of your classroom or school) Toy Speedway. In today's main event, we will compare how fast things move on different surfaces. Let's begin by rolling a Ping-Pong ball on a piece of plain paper (demonstrate with an object and surface from your set of materials). *Now let's roll the Ping-Pong ball on a carpet square* (demonstrate with another surface). Elicit the children's observations and explanations about the relative speed of the object on the two surfaces. Distribute the materials, and say *Ladies and gentlemen, start your speed experiments. Let's see how fast things go.*

Scaffolding Children's Learning
Encourage children to compare the rate of movement based on surface characteristics (e.g., rough or smooth, flat or grooved, wet or dry, slippery or sticky). Inquire about children's reasoning (e.g., *Why do you think it went faster on the shiny fabric?*). Ask them to make and verify predictions. Children may observe rates of speed with their eyes or record actual times. Problem-solve how to compare times (e.g., identify beginning and end points, count the number of seconds). If asked, show children how to use a timing device, or operate it yourself. If they are interested, help them record speeds on the chart.

Children compare how fast objects roll on different surfaces. Here they are rolling Ping-Pong balls on a strip of wood and on a piece of carpet. Next, they'll try some tiles.

Content area:
Science and Technology

Time of day:
Small-group time

Materials
For each child and teacher: An object to roll or slide (e.g., Ping-Pong or golf ball, cylindrical block); 2–3 surfaces to roll or slide objects on (e.g., plain paper, sandpaper, carpet square)

To share: Additional objects to roll or slide (e.g., paper clips, wadded paper balls, plastic lids); other surfaces to roll or slide objects on (e.g., wax paper, crumpled newsprint, oil cloth, felt, corrugated cardboard, plastic tray); stop watch(es) or kitchen timers capable of measuring in seconds

For backup: Chart paper and markers to record speeds under varying conditions

Vocabulary words: *experiment, faster, roll, slide, slower, speed, surface*

Follow-up Ideas

Decide with the children which area of the classroom they want to use to store the objects and surfaces should they want to use them at work (choice) time. Encourage them to explore other conditions that affect speed (e.g., the angle of a ramp, the dampness of an object or surface, whether an object or surface is smooth or bumpy). Post the chart for children to add their observations. Encourage children to explain what conditions they think affect speeds outdoors (e.g., a raindrop sliding down a wall, snow melting off a branch, pulling a wagon across grass or pavement).

What's for Lunch?

36

What Children Do and Learn
Children use their sense of smell to describe and identify a variety of foods.

Story Starter
The children at Magnolia Meadows Day Care Center liked to see what was for lunch every day. If the cook walked by with a jar of tomato sauce, they guessed, "We're having spaghetti." Ask what the children like to eat for lunch. *One day, a new girl named* Fatima *came to the center. She was blind and she couldn't see the food, but she wanted to guess too. What other clues could Fatima use?* Discuss their ideas and say *Fatima guessed by smelling what was for lunch.* Distribute the food items, and say *Let's close our eyes and use our noses to see if we can recognize foods by smell like Fatima did.*

Scaffolding Children's Learning
Encourage children to close their eyes and name foods by smell or identify things they eat that smell like that (e.g., *My daddy puts that on my hotdog*). If children ask, supply the names of foods they do not know. Ask what other foods the smells remind them of and which are used in the foods they eat at home. Pose challenges (e.g., *I'm looking for something that smells like it would go in a fruit salad; I'm thinking of something I eat for breakfast that smells like this. Can you guess what it is?*). Talk about places and experiences children associate with food smells, such as the kitchen, garden, farmer's market, and bakery.

Vocabulary words: aroma, blind, clue, food, scent, smell, spice

Follow-up Ideas
At snacktimes and mealtimes, encourage children to pay attention to the smell of food along with its other properties. Encourage them to guess what they will eat later in the day based on the smells coming from the kitchen. Encourage families to have their children guess what's for breakfast or dinner using their sense of smell. If a child has a stuffy nose (e.g., from a head cold), talk about how it affects his or her sense of smell. Make a "food smell" book for the library using non-perishable items (e.g., dried herbs and spices, fruit rinds). Outside, encourage children to identify the smell of flowers, exhaust fumes, rain, fresh-cut grass, decaying leaves, and so on.

Content area:
Science and Technology

Time of day:
Small-group time

Materials
For each child and teacher: 4–6 foods including those likely to be familiar to the children (e.g., orange rind; banana peel; drops of apple juice in a cup; spoonful of peanut butter, ketchup, or mustard dabbed on paper) and one or two foods that may be less familiar to them (e.g., strawberry, cinnamon, barbeque sauce); include foods and seasonings commonly used by the families in your program

To share: Additional foods (include duplicates and triplicates so children can match items by smell)

For backup: None

8

Art

When you use the Art story starters, children will explore and learn about the following art topics:

- *2-D art materials and tools* — Using art supplies for drawing, painting, print-making, and related media

- *3-D art materials and tools* — Using art supplies for sculpting, building, collaging, and related media

- *Representing with art* — Making accidental and intentional representations of real and imaginary things

- *Art vocabulary* — Learning the words used to talk about art materials, images, techniques, and styles

- *Art appreciation* — Observing and describing art, expressing preferences, exploring art in the community

37 Broken Camera

Content area:
Creative Arts: Art

Time of day:
Small-group time

Materials
For each child and teacher: Paper; drawing materials (e.g., crayons, colored pencils, markers, chalk, charcoal)

To share: None

For backup: None

What Children Do and Learn
Children make representational drawings of a familiar event such as a birthday party.

Story Starter

Pedro was having a birthday party, and the guests wanted to take photographs of him blowing out the candles and opening presents, and of everyone eating cake and ice cream. Talk about the children's experiences with birthday parties. *But when Uncle Louie pushed the button on his camera, nothing happened. The camera was broken!*

Everyone was disappointed until Aunt Selma had an idea: "Let's draw pictures of the party instead." Everyone thought this was a fine idea! Distribute the materials and say *I wonder what you'll draw.* [Note: In place of a birthday party, you can substitute another event of interest to the children, such as a recent field trip.]

Scaffolding Children's Learning

Accept that some children may not draw a party or make a representational drawing. They may choose to explore the materials, how to manipulate them, or the motions their arms make when using them. Let them say what (if anything) they are drawing. Talk about children's choices of materials, colors, lines, shapes, designs, and so on. Describe, and encourage children to describe, their motions as they draw. If children are interested, take dictation or encourage them to write down a story about their picture.

Vocabulary words: *click, disappointed, flash, guest, illustrate, indeed, photographs, suggestion*

During this activity, talk with children about their choices of materials and how they use them to make lines, shapes, and designs.

Follow-up Ideas

Encourage children to represent through their own drawing and paintings the characters and events in familiar picture books, stories, and songs. Draw pictures after a class field trip, a guest visit to the classroom, or other memorable event. Encourage children to draw their plans or represent their work (choice) time activities at recall. Emphasize that the line drawings on the classroom message board stand for objects, people, and events (e.g., ask *What [or who] do you think this is a picture of?*). Talk about how daily routine posters, area signs, labels for materials, and so on are drawings that represent or stand for something. Look at reproductions of paintings and sculptures, and ask the children what they think the artist meant to show.

38 Cave Art

Content area:
Creative Arts: Art

Time of day:
Small-group time

Materials
*For each child
and teacher:*
Reproduction
of a painting or
photograph that
features sharp
contrasts, and
different colors
and degrees of
brightness (light
and shadow);
flashlight

To share: Heavy
sheets or blankets
draped over a table
to make a "cave";
if possible, locate
the cave (move
the table) near a
window with lots
of natural light
coming in

For backup:
Additional pictures,
drawing materials

What Children Do and Learn

Children look at artwork in daylight and then with a flashlight in the dark, exploring the different effects of lighting.

Story Starter

One sunny afternoon, Rosie the Bear painted a picture that she liked so much she took it to bed with her in her cave that night. But it was dark inside the cave. How could Rosie see her picture in the dark? Ask for the children's ideas. *Rosie had a flashlight in her cave to shine on her painting. "I wonder if it will look the same with the flashlight as it did in the daylight," she said. What do you think?* Look at one or two pictures with the children in the daylight and talk about the brightness of the colors, light, and shadow. Give each child a picture and a flashlight, crawl into the cave, and say *I wonder how your pictures will look inside our cave.*

A sheet or blanket draped over a table creates a "cave" in which children can explore the effects of light and shadow.

Scaffolding Children's Learning

Encourage children to compare colors and contrasts in daylight versus in the dark with flashlights. For children who are primarily interested in using the flashlights, talk about the light and shadow effects they create on the floor and on the walls of the cave. Encourage children to move in and out of the cave, or lift and lower one edge of the sheet or blanket, to observe the effects of the light. If children are interested, provide drawing materials so they can look at the effect of light and dark on their own artwork.

Vocabulary words: *bright, dark, daylight, flashlight, light, shadow*

Follow-up Ideas

Encourage children to look at their own artwork in different lighting conditions, including outdoors, at different times of day, under fluorescent and incandescent light, or beneath or behind furniture that blocks or filters light. Outdoors, look at the same object in light and shadow (e.g., the green of leaves on a bush partly in sun and partly in shade). Provide flashlights so children can experiment with the effects of lighting on various objects and motions. Provide books with photographs, sculptures, or other images in which light and shadow are an important component. Share photos of stage sets that use lighting to create dramatic effects.

39 Classroom Collage

Content area:
Creative Arts: Art

Time of day:
Small-group time

Materials
For each child and teacher: Glue stick

To share: Roll of paper long enough for children to each have 2 feet of workspace; collage materials (e.g., wood scraps, white and colored paper scraps, beads, shells, dried pasta, birdseed, leaves, twigs, pine cones, seed pods, ribbons, yarn, packaging pellets, string, pieces of fabric, buttons, bottle caps, foil)

For backup: Additional collage and fastening materials (e.g., tape, staplers, paste, glue); sheets of paper if children want to make their own collages

What Children Do and Learn
Children explore a variety of three-dimensional (3-D) materials while collaborating on a group collage.

Story Starter
Walking to school one day, Benny saw red and yellow leaves stuck to a fence. He added some orange leaves he found on the ground. On his way home, Benny saw someone had added twigs and acorns to the fence. The next day, people brought beads and buttons, flower petals, scraps of paper and cloth, and added those items to the fence too. It was a neighborhood collage! Talk with the children about what a collage is, and solicit their ideas about other materials that could be added. Show them the materials, help them spread out along the roll of paper, and say *I wonder what our classroom collage will look like.*

Scaffolding Children's Learning
Talk about the properties of the materials children choose and how they arrange and attach them. Some children may want to make their own collages instead of working on the class collage. Others may explore but not attach the materials. Support all these initiatives. Encourage children to stand back now and then to look at the collage as a whole. Ask children how they obtained certain effects (e.g., *How did you make it smooth on the bottom and rough along the top?*). Display the collage where parents can see it at dropoff and pickup times. Attach a work-in-progress sign if children want to continue creating the collage at work (choice) time. Take a picture, or a series of pictures, for a class book or family newsletter.

Vocabulary words: added, collage, fence, neighborhood, scraps

Follow-up Ideas
Provide a variety of collage materials, bases (e.g., paper, wood blocks), and fasteners in the art area. At cleanup time, ask children whether materials can be added to the collage supplies instead of being thrown out (e.g., cut-up pieces of paper used as play money). Encourage families to bring in scrap materials. Go on a neighborhood walk to collect materials from nature and use these to make a collage at small- or large-group time, indoors or outdoors. Read storybooks that feature collages as illustrations (e.g., *Snowballs* by Lois Ehlert). Look for reproductions of collage artwork in postcards, art magazines, and exhibit brochures.

Ice Sculptures

What Children Do and Learn
Children explore the properties of wet, moldable snow and use it to make sculptures and carvings with various tools.

Story Starter
The Good Witch of the North lived in a very cold place. Everything was made of snow and ice. Talk about the children's experiences with snow and ice. *The witch lived in a big ice palace but all the rooms were empty. It was boring! So she flew on her ice broom to the North Pole and brought back ice sculptures to fill it. Some were made by molding.* Shape a mound of snow with your hands. *Others sculptures were made by carving.* Demonstrate using a carving tool. Distribute the materials, and say *There are still many empty rooms in the ice palace. I wonder what you will sculpt with your mounds of snow and ice.* [Note: If there is no snow in your climate, replace the "ice palace" with a "sand castle" in the story, and use wet sand in place of snow.]

Scaffolding Children's Learning
Talk with children about the qualities of the snow (e.g., appearance, texture, temperature, smell), their actions, the tools they use, and the effects they create as they explore the snow. Expect the children to use the snow in different ways, including simple exploration (e.g., feeling it, poking fingers or twigs into it, spreading it on the ground), molding shapes, carving impressions, or creating representations of people, animals, or objects. Encourage children to mix in dirt and describe its effects on the snow's appearance, texture, and moldability. Provide food coloring and decorations for those interested in adding these materials to their sculptures.

Vocabulary words: carve, cold, ice sculpture, mold, mound, surface

Follow-up Ideas
Observe and discuss with children what happens to their sculptures in the next few days (e.g., do they remain frozen, melt into interesting new shapes, smooth out, or develop new depressions?). At dropoff and pickup times, encourage children to talk with their parents about how they made the sculptures. Provide other 3-D art materials (e.g., clay, play dough, beeswax, wet sand) so children can compare their properties. Ask children which materials are easier or harder to mold or carve, which are wetter or drier, and which ones hold their shape better. At outside time, talk with children about the structures and objects they make with snow, wet sand, and mud.

Content area:
Creative Arts: Art

Time of day:
Small-group time (held outside, preferably after a wet snow when it is most moldable)

Materials
For each child and teacher: Tool for sculpting and carving (e.g., pail and shovel, wooden dowel, treaded tire on toy vehicle, cooking utensil); mound of snow approximately 12" around (if snow is not available in your climate, you may be able to obtain some from local ice arenas that clear their rinks)

To share: Additional tools for sculpting and carving

For backup: Dirt, food coloring; decorations (e.g., buttons, shells)

41 Imprints in Clay

Content area:
Creative Arts: Art

Time of day:
Small-group time

Materials
For each child and teacher: Small ball of modeling clay (or play dough)

To share: Materials of different sizes, patterns, and textures to make impressions (imprints) (e.g., wheeled toys, forks, straws, pegs, toothpicks, Lego blocks, pipe cleaners, chopsticks, shells, bark, combs, paper clips, canvas or wire mesh, shoelaces, patterned shoe soles, buttons, feathers), hardware (e.g., screws, nuts, bolts)

For backup: Rolling pins, dowels, or other tools to flatten the clay

What Children Do and Learn
Children explore the impressions that materials of different sizes, patterns, and textures leave in clay.

Story Starter
Monday it rained. Tuesday it rained again. What do you think happened on Wednesday? Pause for the children to answer. *Jimmy and Jessie missed going outside to play.* Talk about how the children feel when they cannot play outside because of the rain. *Jimmy and Jessie were so happy when the sun came back out. The ground was still wet so they put on their boots and went for a walk. They saw tire tracks in the mud.* Flatten a piece of clay and make a tread mark with a wheeled toy. *They saw a bird's footprints.* Make a bird's footprint with a toothpick. *Jessie looked down and saw their footprints. Then Jimmy made an impression of his hand in the mud!* Make your handprint in a flat piece of clay. Distribute the materials, and say *I wonder what prints you will make.*

In this activity, children can use their hands and different tools to make marks and imprints in clay. This child used a chopstick to make straight lines.

Scaffolding Children's Learning

If needed, help children flatten balls of clay using their hands or with tools. Encourage them to try different imprint materials and to manipulate (handle) them in different ways. Describe, and encourage children to describe, the materials they use and the imprint effects they get. Imitate what they do, and ask them for directions so you can get the same effects (e.g., *Tell me how to make a mark like yours. What did you use? How did you move it?*). Ask children to guess which material(s) you or their peers used to make marks.

Vocabulary words: *flatten, footprint, handprint, impression, tire track*

Follow-up Ideas

Provide imprinting materials in the art area. Bring them outside. After it rains, or you add water to a patch of earth, encourage children to explore imprints made by items from nature and to guess what made them. Go for a walk after it rains to look for imprints. Take photos to post on the wall or in a book. Encourage children to make labels identifying different imprinting materials.

42 Mirror, Mirror

Content area:
Creative Arts: Art

Time of day:
Small-group time

Materials
For each child and teacher: Hand-held mirror, paper, drawing materials (e.g., crayons, markers, colored pencils)

To share: None

For backup: Extra paper; collage materials to represent physical features (e.g., yarn for hair, sequins for freckles)

What Children Do and Learn
Children look at themselves in mirrors, describe their features, and draw their self-portraits.

Story Starter
Janie had never met her cousin Sasha because they lived far apart. One day Janie's mother said, "Sasha is coming to visit us. We'll pick her up at the airport." Janie was excited but worried. "How will I know what Sasha looks like? And how will she recognize me?" Solicit the children's ideas. *Janie said, "I know! We can draw pictures of ourselves and mail them to each another." She drew a circle for her face and her curly red hair. But she couldn't think what else to draw. "I know," she said. "I'll look in the mirror and then I can draw what I look like."* Hand out mirrors for children to look at themselves and talk about what they see. Distribute the drawing materials and say *I wonder what pictures you'll draw of yourselves.*

Scaffolding Children's Learning
Encourage children to look at themselves in the mirror before they begin to draw. Ask them to talk about the facial features they observe (e.g., *What shape is your mouth? How is your nose different than mine? I wonder who has light-colored eyes and who has dark eyes*). The more they observe their features, the more detailed their drawings will be. Accept that some children may only look in the mirror, make nonrepresentational drawings (scribbles, shapes, designs), and/or draw things other than themselves. Explain that a person's picture is called a *portrait,* and when artists draw themselves, it is called a *self-portrait.* Encourage children who are interested to make portraits of you or other children, and to incorporate the collage materials.

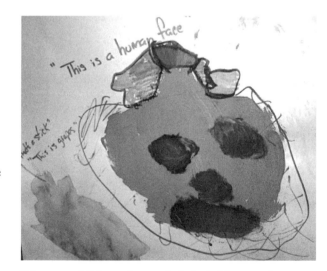

The more children observe their facial features in a mirror, the more detailed their self-portraits will be. This child drew every feature and topped it with a fancy hat.

Vocabulary words: *curly, dark-colored, light-colored, mirror, portrait, recognize*

Follow-up Ideas

Display portraits in the classroom. Make a book for the class library. Encourage children to draw portraits of family members and add these to the book. For another small-group time, take photos of the children as the basis for drawing self-portraits. Use children's features as the basis for transitions, beginning with one trait and incorporating more details later in the year (e.g., *Whoever has brown eyes, put on your coat to go outside; Whoever has brown eyes and straight black hair…; Whoever has black hair in braids with blue rubber bands…;* and so on).

43 Museum Exhibit

Content area:
Creative Arts: Art

Time of day:
Small-group time

Materials
For each child and teacher: None

To share: A collection of 2-D and 3-D artwork (e.g., drawings, paintings, ceramics, photography, weaving, beadwork, jewelry, and postcard reproductions or models [include artwork made by the children, and objects brought in by parents]); paper or index cards; and writing tools to make labels

For backup: Other museum and/or exhibit props (e.g., blocks or inverted boxes to serve as pedestals, sheets of colored paper on which to display artwork)

What Children Do and Learn
Children make a museum exhibit by sorting and arranging, labeling, and describing the properties of various two-dimensional (2-D) and three-dimensional (3-D) artworks. (This activity is best done after a field trip to a museum, gallery, art fair, or artist's studio.)

Story Starter
A new art museum opened in the city and artists brought in their artwork for the first exhibit. They had paintings, drawings, ceramic pots, and weavings. Discuss with the children the other types of artwork you have, relating it to a recent field trip or experiences with their families. *The museum director said, "I wonder how I can sort and label all this artwork. For example, I could put all the artwork that's flat in one gallery and everything that stands up in another.* Group a few items this way, accepting children's ideas. *Or I could separate bright things that make you feel happy and dark things that make you feel sad.* Group several items on this dimension. Distribute the materials and say *I wonder how you will arrange your art exhibit.*

Scaffolding Children's Learning
Talk with the children about the items they choose and how they arrange them. Encourage them to describe the artwork and their basis for sorting (e.g., by formal properties such as color and size, type of material or technique used, feelings the artwork evokes). Talk about the difference between two- and three-dimensional artwork, and whether the art portrays something real (pictures of objects, people, or events) or abstract (colors, lines, shapes, designs). Midway through the activity, invite children to make labels like the ones in the museum (help them as needed). Discuss the information they want to put on their labels (e.g., title, name of artist, materials and techniques, where and when the artwork was made).

Vocabulary words: *two-dimensional (2-D), three-dimensional (3-D), artist, exhibit, gallery, museum*

Follow-up Ideas
Decide with the children where to store the artwork collection and labeling supplies for availability at work (choice) time. Provide work-in-progress signs. Bring in reproductions of artwork (e.g., postcards, exhibit brochures), and encourage children to talk about the properties of the artwork represented. Look at and talk about the qualities of the artwork in familiar storybooks (it is easier for children to talk about the illustrations if they are already familiar with the story). Read books about artists written for young children.

Painting Dog Houses

44

What Children Do and Learn

Children explore the effects of using brushes of different sizes (widths) and painting tools made of other materials as they paint with water.

Story Starter

Once there were three dogs: a tiny dog, a middle-size dog, and a huge dog. They liked to play together so they built doghouses next to one another: a tiny house for the tiny dog, a middle-size house for the middle-size dog, and for the huge dog, a ___ house. Pause for the children to share their ideas. With water and a thin brush, outline a small square "house" on the pavement. Solicit the children's ideas on how to make the other two houses (e.g., house size and shape, brush size). *Then the three dogs painted the walls of their houses. They each chose which size brush to use and decided whether to paint with other tools as well.* Distribute the materials, point out the other tools, and say *I wonder what you'll paint on the pavement and what brushes and tools you'll use.*

Children experiment with different widths of brushes and thicknesses of paint as they cover the paper and observe the varied textural effects they get.

Content area:
Creative Arts: Art

Time of day:
Small-group time (done outdoors on pavement, on the side of the building, or on the surface of a picnic table; or carry sheets of butcher paper outdoors to spread on the ground)

Materials
For each child and teacher: Brushes in three different widths; bucket or other container to fill with water (container should be at least as wide as the widest brush)

To share: Other painting tools (e.g., brushes in other sizes, shapes, or thicknesses [round or "bushy" and flat or "thin" bristles; straight-edged and pointed tip], sponges of various widths and thicknesses, rags of different sizes and materials, and squeeze tools such as basters and eyedroppers)

For backup: Extra buckets, painting tools, and butcher paper

Scaffolding Children's Learning

Encourage children to help one another fill and carry their buckets to the surface where they will paint. Some may choose to simply play with the water or explore the brushes and other tools without painting anything. Discuss the dimensions of the houses or whatever else children paint, and the size (width and thickness) of the painting tools they use. Encourage them to explore other tools and to describe their visual effects, such as the width of a mark or whether an edge is smooth or fuzzy. Ask children how you can get the same effects, using questions like *What tool did you use? How long did you soak the sponge in the water? Did you squeeze it first? How hard should I press?* Comment on how much water each tool absorbs and leaves behind. Describe, and encourage children to describe, how they vary their gestures with the type of tool they use.

Vocabulary words: *bristle, huge, middle-size, pavement, press, squeeze, tiny*

Follow-up Ideas

Provide drawing and painting tools in a wide variety of sizes and shapes in the art area. Store them in buckets if children want to carry them outdoors at outside time. As children draw and paint at work (choice) or small-group time, talk with them about the effects of the materials and actions they use.

Sammy Squirrel's House

45

What Children Do and Learn
Children look at photos of houses, describing the different architectural features they see, then use construction materials to build their own houses.

Story Starter
Sammy Squirrel collected so many nuts that they were piled on top of the bed, pushed under the couch, and rolling off the table. Sammy said, "I need a bigger house." He scampered all around town with his camera, taking pictures of houses. Then he looked at them to decide what kind of house he wanted to build. Look at several house photos with the children. Encourage them to describe and discuss various features (e.g., size, how many families live there, number of windows, building materials, roof lines, types of porches and walkways, whether there is a garage). Ask the children *What kind of house do you think Sammy will build? Why?* Discuss their reasons. Spread out the photos, distribute the building materials, and say *I wonder what kinds of houses you will build.*

Scaffolding Children's Learning
Encourage children to refer to or look at the photos to get ideas for their constructions. Describe, and encourage children to describe, architectural features of the houses in the photos and the houses they build (e.g., where the door is located, number of windows, whether there's a driveway and/or garage). Talk about how the houses they make are the same as or different from those in the photos. Ask children about their own homes and how the architectural features compare to those in the photos. Encourage them to collaborate and to help one another solve construction problems.

Vocabulary words: *apartment building, downspout, roof, railing, scamper, windowpane*

Follow-up Ideas
Take a neighborhood walk and talk about the features of the houses. Invite families to send in photos of their houses, and post these in the art area and block area as an inspiration for the children's drawings and constructions. From a safe position, observe a local construction site at various points during the building process. Document its progress with photos. Talk about the architectural characteristics of the houses pictured in magazines, building supply catalogs, "home improvement" supplements, and familiar storybooks.

Content area:
Creative Arts: Art

Time of day:
Small-group time

Materials
For each child and teacher: Construction materials (unit blocks, Legos, modeling clay, play dough)

To share: Photos of different houses (from magazines, advertisements, and so on) in a range of sizes and styles, such as single-family homes, duplexes, apartment buildings, and garden apartments (include houses and buildings representative of those the children live in as well as styles they may not have seen before)

For backup: Architectural magazines; storybooks that feature diverse and interesting looking houses

46 Statue Zoo

Content area:
Creative Arts: Art

Time of day:
Small-group time

Materials
For each child and teacher: Ball of clay 4"–5" in diameter; a sculpting or carving tool (e.g., plastic eating utensils, chopsticks, rolling pins or wooden dowels, garlic presses, combs, golf tees, nails and screws, paper clips, screwdrivers, scissors, twigs); sturdy base to work on and move finished sculptures (e.g., plywood slab, heavy cardboard, plastic tray); plastic to cover sculptures while they dry

To share: Additional sculpting and carving tools

For backup: None

What Children Do and Learn
Children explore the properties of clay, and sculpting and carving tools, while making statues of animals, people, and objects they might find at the zoo.

Story Starter
Kobe was walking down the street when he saw a sign that said, "This way to the Statue Zoo." He was very curious to find out what a Statue Zoo was! Talk with the children about what they think it might be. *Kobe went up to the ticket booth. It was made of clay. He bought a ticket and that was made of clay too!* Form a piece of clay into a small ticket-shaped rectangle. *Inside the Statue Zoo, he saw tigers, monkeys, and giraffes. Guess what! They were all statues made of clay too!* Talk with the children about what other animals might be in the Statue Zoo, and whether they would move or make animal sounds. *When Kobe got tired, he sat on a clay bench. He drank from a clay water fountain and even ate a clay hot dog when he got hungry!* Give each child a ball of clay and set of tools, and say *I wonder what things Kobe will find in your Statue Zoo.*

Scaffolding Children's Learning
Talk about the properties of clay and the tools the children use. Encourage them to explore the clay with their hands and to describe its properties (e.g., color, moisture, density, temperature). Discuss children's actions and the effects of using different tools on the size, shape, and surface texture of the clay. Accept that some children may just explore the clay and tools while others will make clay objects (including things not found at a zoo). Move the finished sculptures to a safe place where children can watch them dry, covered with plastic to minimize cracking.

Vocabulary words: flatten, gouge, puncture, squishy, stand still, statue

Follow-up Ideas
With the children, periodically check the sculptures as they dry to observe changes in color, size (shrinkage), and moistness. Provide clay and tools in the art area. At another small-group time, provide finished sculptures for children to use in making up and acting out their own scenarios. Put them in the toy area with other small animals made of different materials (e.g., wood, plastic, stuffed fabric). Bring in photos and postcards showing sculptures of animals and people. Solicit children's ideas on how they were made.

What's It About?

What Children Do and Learn
Children look at realistic and abstract art and describe what they think the pictures are about.

Story Starter
Dan and Dora went to the art museum. There were lots of different rooms, called galleries, *and each had a different type of art. Dan walked into a gallery that said Realistic Art. Here is one of the pictures (or sculptures) he saw. What do you think it's about?* Discuss an example of representational art with the children, pointing out that it's an image of a "real thing" (a person or object). *Dora looked in another gallery labeled Abstract Art. What do you suppose the artist wants to say here?* Discuss an example of abstract (nonfigurative) art, emphasizing that it just has colors, shapes, and/or lines. *Here's some other artwork Dan and Dora saw at the museum.* Hand out the pictures and say *I wonder what you think about each of these.*

Content area:
Creative Arts: Art

Time of day:
Small-group time

Materials
For each child and teacher:
1–2 pictures of representational (realistic or figurative) art and 1–2 pictures of abstract (nonfigurative) art (e.g., postcard reproductions, pictures from art magazines, exhibit brochures)

To share: Additional pictures including postcards, art books, and museum and exhibit brochures

For backup: Drawing materials

In this follow-up activity, children are encouraged to draw their own figurative or abstract works of art for a class mural.

Scaffolding Children's Learning

Talk about what the children think is conveyed in each picture. Accept their interpretations and preferences. There are no right or wrong answers. Some children will focus on one or two details, others on the picture as a whole. They may comment on color, shape, image, shadow, size, medium, technique, or mood (emotional tone). Discuss whatever captures their attention. Talk about whether an image or style reminds them of things in their own life, such as activities, people, characters in books and songs, and colors or patterns at home or in the classroom. Encourage them to draw their own figurative or abstract work of art.

Vocabulary words: *abstract, background, foreground, image, medium, realistic*

Follow-up Ideas

Display reproductions of artwork throughout the classroom and at the children's eye level. Include realistic and abstract representations and various media, techniques, and styles (e.g., photographs, oils, watercolors, pastels, collages, cartoons, stick figures, color and black-and-white images). Encourage them to connect their own artwork to these images. Put storybooks, art books, and magazines featuring different types of art in the book area. After children are familiar with the story, focus on the illustrations in books. Encourage them to describe what they see, and what it makes them think about or feel. Visit an art museum (plan the trip ahead of time with a docent), and choose a selected variety of artworks to study and discuss with the children. Invite artists who do different types of work to visit the classroom or host children in their studios.

Where Can I Draw?

What Children Do and Learn
Children explore the effects of drawing with a crayon on surfaces made of different materials, colors, and textures.

Story Starter
Fiona loved to draw with crayons. Red was her favorite color. Where could she draw? She couldn't do it on her bedroom wall because it made her parents angry. She couldn't draw on the lampshade. Where else was Fiona not allowed to draw? Solicit children's ideas. *Fiona got very frustrated. "Where can I draw?" she asked. Her parents gave her paper and wood scraps* (point to and name several materials). *Fiona was happy! She drew and drew, and her red crayon looked different on every surface.* Distribute the materials, and say *I wonder what you'll draw on with your crayon and how it will look.*

Scaffolding Children's Learning
Talk with children about the different surfaces (e.g., whether they are light or dark, plain or coated, rough or smooth). Describe, and encourage children to describe, how the color or texture of the crayon appears different depending on the drawing surface (e.g., whether it looks brighter or duller against a light or dark background, whether the line is smooth or bumpy on flat or textured paper). Talk about whether the type of surface affects the speed, pressure, or their other actions with the crayon.

Vocabulary words: *coated, corrugated, matte, pressure, scrub, slick, uncoated*

Follow-up Ideas
Provide a variety of paper and other drawing surfaces in the art area, including recyclables donated by parents and staff. Encourage the children to close their eyes, feel the surfaces with their hands, and describe the different sensations they experience. Ask them to predict the visual and textural effects of drawing on different surfaces and to compare the actual effects with their predictions. Visit a local gallery or studio to see the painting and drawing surfaces artists use, including canvas, paper, wood, fiber, ceramics, stone, plastic, and glass.

Content area:
Creative Arts: Art

Time of day:
Small-group time

Materials
For each child and teacher: Wax crayon in a primary color (e.g., red, blue, or yellow); two drawing surfaces, such as different kinds of paper (e.g., white or brown butcher paper, colored construction paper, lined or ruled paper, graph paper, coated fingerpaint paper, wax paper, newsprint, gift wrap); cardboard (e.g., flat, corrugated); foil; wood scraps; fabric (e.g., felt, cotton, rayon); plastic lids

To share: Additional drawing surfaces

For backup: Crayons in secondary colors (e.g., green, orange, purple)

9

Pretend Play

The areas of learning that young children will explore with Pretend Play story starters include:

- *Representing sights and sounds* — Imitating actions and sounds

- *Representing people and actions* — Pretending and role-playing real and imaginary situations

- *Drama vocabulary* — Learning the words used to talk about "acting out" character and narrative

- *Drama appreciation* — Learning about people and activities in dramatic media (e.g., theater, film, television)

49 All Kinds of Kitties

Content area:
Creative Arts:
Pretend Play

Time of day:
Large-group time

Materials
For each child and teacher: None

To share: None

For backup: Props that pets might use, such as bowls, blankets, balls, string (for leashes)

What Children Do and Learn
Children pretend to be kittens available for adoption at the animal shelter and act out their personalities.

Story Starter
Mimi was excited. Today she was going to the animal shelter to adopt a kitten. There were a lot of kittens to choose from so she asked the shelter worker to describe each one's personality. One was named Sleepy Kitty *because it always yawned, stretched its legs, and nodded off to sleep.* Act out these gestures. *Another was dubbed* Spinning Kitty *because it chased its tail in a circle before it curled up on the floor.* Act out these gestures. *There was also a kitten named* Very Hungry Kitty. *Why do you suppose that was its name?* Solicit the children's ideas, and say *Let's pretend to be kittens too. I wonder what kinds of personalities you will have.*

Scaffolding Children's Learning
Encourage children to name, describe, and act out the personality traits of different kittens. Imitate their vocalizations and behaviors. Listen, observe, and make comments such as *Felicia says her name is* Bouncy Kitty. *She's bending and straightening her knees to make her body go up and down, up and down.* Accept the choices of children who act out other kinds of animals (e.g., puppies, guinea pigs) and encourage their role play. Act out a personality and say *Can you guess what the name of my kitty is?* Have the children act out a type of kitten (or pet of their choice) without naming it so you and the others can guess what its name is.

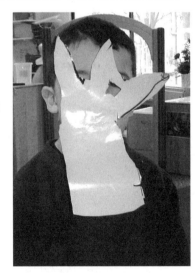

As a follow-up to this activity, teachers can provide art materials for children to represent kittens and other kinds of animals.

Vocabulary words: *adopt, animal shelter, dubbed (as in "named"), nod off, personality*

Follow-up Ideas

Provide art materials for children to represent different kinds of kittens. Ask about their pets' personalities. If there are classroom pets, discuss their personalities (e.g., how they act, what sounds they make, whether they eat and drink fast or slow, if they like to be held or if they are shy). Encourage children to describe trips to the local animal shelter, kittens they've seen for adoption at the farmer's market, and related experiences. Read books that feature animals as characters, and talk with the children about the characters' traits.

50 Dinosaur Stew

Content area:
Creative Arts:
Pretend Play

Time of day:
Small-group time

Materials
For each child and teacher: Ball of play dough, bowl, stirring spoon, plastic knife

To share: Pots and pans, rolling pins, aprons, pot holders, measuring cups and spoons, spatulas, graters, garlic presses, plastic containers with lids

For backup: Clean and empty food containers, spice containers

What Children Do and Learn
Children pretend to cook, serve, and store leftover food by making stew for dinosaurs and other animals.

Story Starter
After a long day roaming the earth, the dinosaurs were very hungry. Their stomachs growled and gurgled, and rumbled and roared. Ask if the children's stomachs ever growl and how it sounds and feels. *The dinosaurs decided to cook a huge pot of dinosaur stew for dinner. They put big meatballs and a spoonful of little peas in the pot and stirred it up.* Put large and small balls of play dough in the bowl and stir them with a spoon. Pretend to taste the stew. *"This tastes bland," said one dinosaur. "It needs pepper to spice it up."* Pretend to shake in some pepper. Distribute the materials, and say *I wonder what you'll put in your dinosaur stew.*

Scaffolding Children's Learning
Encourage children to create, name, and mix the stew ingredients. Describe, and encourage children to describe, their actions and the features of the kitchen utensils they are using (e.g., *Kelly made a mound of grated carrots*). Talk about foods and seasonings that are part of children's meals at home (e.g., *Vinod stirred lentils into his stew*). Suggest and invite suggestions for side dishes: *I dunk bread to soak up the juices. What do you like to eat with your dinosaur stew?* "Taste" what they cook and make requests (e.g., *May I please have a smaller portion; This tastes underdone, I think it needs to cook longer*). Elaborate on the story (e.g., *Other animals wanted to eat stew too. The squirrels added acorns and dried leaves to the pot. I wonder who else came and what they added*). If children want to store the stew to use at work (choice) time, encourage them to put it into plastic containers.

Vocabulary words: bland, dunk, growl, gurgle, roaming, spice, stew

Follow-up Ideas
Stock the house area with a variety of kitchen utensils and clean, empty food containers. Include tools and foods that are familiar to children from the dishes they eat at home (e.g., rice steamer, tortilla press, empty pasta box, hummus container). Ask families to contribute old cooking utensils and empty containers. As children role-play cooking in the house area, talk to them about the ingredients they use and the techniques they use in cooking. Encourage children to use cooking utensils with 2-D and 3-D art materials.

Down Came the Snow

51

Content area:
Creative Arts:
Pretend Play

Time of day:
Large-group time

Materials
For each child and teacher: None

To share: None

For backup: None

What Children Do and Learn
Children change the words to a familiar rhyme and act out the variations.

Story Starter
Begin by saying and acting out a familiar rhyme with the children, such as "The Eensy Weensy Spider." Then continue with the story. *One day the eensy weensy spider went up the water spout. It was relaxing in the sun, when all of a sudden down came the snow!* (Or use another weather condition common to your area.) Move your fingers like snow coming down, and encourage the children to imitate the movement. *The eensy weensy spider said, "Brrr, I'm freezing!" It shivered and its teeth chattered.* Shiver, chatter your teeth, and wrap your arms around yourself. Encourage children to do the same and act out other ways of being cold. *At last the sun came back out. What do you think the spider did then?* Solicit, repeat, and act out the children's ideas. *I wonder what else will happen to that poor eensy weensy spider!*

Building on the children's familiarity with a popular rhyme, such as "The Eensy Weensy Spider," the adult invites children to change the words and act out the variations.

Scaffolding Children's Learning

Repeat the chant, each time inviting children's variations. In addition to changing what happens to the weather, they may have the spider do something other than climb the spout. Encourage children to experiment with different actions (e.g., *How else could we show the spider is wet [or cold or hot]?*). If children run out of ideas, suggest a new variation (e.g., the eensy weensy spider went down the slide) or character (e.g., the roly-poly worm). Accept children's ideas and encourage their imaginative suggestions. If necessary, repeat and clarify what they say and do so the others understand and can pick up on their ideas.

Vocabulary words: *brrr, chatter, freezing, relaxing, shiver, weather*

Follow-up Ideas

Repeat this activity with other familiar rhymes, chants, and songs. At large-group time, encourage children to choose a song from the class song book and then add the variations they create. Provide art materials during small-group time for children to represent these variations. Take pictures and encourage children to guess (remember) which variation they were acting out. Invite children to vary a familiar rhyme as a way to move to the next activity during transitions.

Field Trip Follow-Up

52

What Children Do and Learn

Children re-enact a class field trip, recalling what happened and elaborating on it by adding events they imagine. (This activity is best done a day or two after a class field trip.)

Story Starter

(This story starter is based on a field trip to a fruit farm. Adapt the story to fit your class trip.) *Yesterday, our class went to visit the ___ Fruit Farm. Everyone took a basket to collect fruit.* Give each child a basket. *Time to get on the bus.* With the children, act out getting on the bus. Encourage them to use props to make a bus, line up the seats, and so on. *What happened on the bus?* Solicit and act out their ideas. *Uh, oh! The driver is heading in the opposite direction from the farm. We're lost. What should we do?* Solicit and act out their ideas. *Whew! We got straightened out. Okay, we finally made it to the fruit farm. What happens now?*

Scaffolding Children's Learning

Encourage the children to remember actual events from their field trip and/or to use their imaginations to suggest and act out what might have happened. Repeat what they say, clarifying if necessary so everyone can understand. Encourage children to act out events from the trip in their own way, and to imitate and elaborate on one another's ideas. Use props to reenact events. Comment on what children do (e.g., *Felicia is putting peaches in her basket; Jeremy and Rachel are hungry. They're sitting under a shady tree to eat their sack lunches*). Make occasional comments (e.g., *Do you remember what happened after we tasted the blueberries? Suppose it started to rain. How would we walk through the berry field then?*).

Vocabulary words: direction, field, opposite, sack, shady, straightened out

Follow-up Ideas

At small-group time, provide 2-D and 3-D art materials for children to represent the field trip. Make a book with photos of the trip, add the children's drawings, and put it in the book area. Encourage children to share the book with parents at dropoff and pickup times. Put copies of the photos on the parents' bulletin board. Bring in books, magazines, catalogs, and other printed materials featuring fruits and farming. Provide gardening equipment in the classroom and for outdoor play. Write a group "thank you" note to the people at the fruit farm with children writing and/or drawing things they remember from the trip. Act out other field trips (e.g., a neighborhood walk, a visit to the pumpkin patch or pet store) with words, actions, and props.

Content area:
Creative Arts:
Pretend Play

Time of day:
Large-group time

Materials
For each child and teacher: Small basket (or other easily carried container)

To share: Props to re-enact the trip, such as blocks or chairs to represent the bus and seats, paper bags for sack lunches, dress-up clothes for farm workers (e.g., boots and straw hats), plastic fruit or blocks to collect in baskets, and so on

For backup: Photos from the trip, pictures of fruit from magazines and seed catalogs

53 Going Fishing

Content area:
Creative Arts:
Pretend Play

Time of day:
Small-group time

Materials
For each child and teacher: Fishing pole (e.g., magnetic wand, or wooden stick with yarn or string for the "line," and a magnet at the end of the line for the "hook"); basket

To share: Pieces of paper in different sizes and shapes, attached to paper clips and spread around the table for children to "catch" (insert a paper clip through a hole in the corner of each shape so the magnetic "hook" will pick it up)

For backup: Large pieces of blue paper or fabric to make a "lake"

What Children Do and Learn
Children use magnetic poles to "fish" for unusual and imaginary objects at the bottom of a mystery "lake."

Story Starter
Louisa and Paul took their fishing poles to Mystery Lake. Why do you suppose it was called Mystery Lake? Solicit the children's ideas. *At Mystery Lake, you never knew what you would catch. Louisa dunked her fishing pole in the water and caught a birdhouse. She put it in their basket.* Use your "pole" to catch a piece of paper and put it in your basket. *Paul lowered his hook in the lake and pulled out an airplane!* Catch something else, struggle to reel it in, and put it in the basket. *"There sure are odd things at the bottom of Mystery Lake!" exclaimed Louisa. "I wonder what other strange things we'll catch," pondered Paul.* Distribute the materials, and say *Let's see what you'll catch when you go fishing in Mystery Lake.*

Scaffolding Children's Learning
Encourage children to imagine what they will catch and to pretend pieces of paper are various objects. Children may say they are catching fish or that they caught the same objects as you. Describe your objects and encourage children to describe theirs (e.g., *It's a birdhouse with a tiny hole for little birds to get inside. Did you catch a birdhouse too? What does yours look like?*). Talk about the motions of fishing, including how children put the line in the water and pull something out, and how they remove an object and put it in the basket. Encourage them to tell about fishing with their families (e.g., where they go, what the rods look and feel like, what they use as bait, what they catch, what they do with the fish, and so on) and/or fishing experiences they've heard or read about (e.g., in books, songs, movies).

Vocabulary words: bait, bob, dunk, hook, odd, mystery, reel in

Follow-up Ideas
Ask children where to store the fishing poles and other fishing materials should they want to use them at work (choice) time. Bury metallic objects in the sand table or in the sandbox outside if children want to "fish" for them. For planning and recall time, make area signs with paper clips attached at the corners, and have children "fish" for the area where they will (or did) play. Provide unlabeled shapes, and encourage the children to fish for and name the objects they will (or did) use in that area.

Here Comes the Train

What Children Do and Learn

Children make the motions and sounds of a train as it travels over different terrain and stops to pick up passengers and cargo.

Content area:
Creative Arts:
Pretend Play

Time of day:
Large-group time

Materials
For each child and teacher: None

To share: None

For backup: None

Story Starter

Chugga, chugga (or other train sound.) *Whoo-hee* (or other whistle sound). *Here comes the train, pulling into the station. "All aboard" shouts the conductor.* Lift your legs as though climbing aboard a train and invite the children to do the same. (They do not need to line up like a train. Have them spread out so they can move freely.) *When all the passengers are on board, the conductor blows the whistle.* Encourage the children to make a whistle sound. *Then the train exits the station and picks up speed. It's going faster and faster.* Slap your thighs and say *chugga, chugga* increasingly faster. Invite the children to suggest other actions and words to show the train picking up speed. *Whoa! There's a hill ahead. It's going to slow us down.* Get the children's ideas on how to slow down, and then say *I wonder where else the train will take us on its journey.*

Scaffolding Children's Learning

Suggest other places and actions for the train, and ask children for their ideas. For example, go through a tunnel (flick the lights on and off), go around a curve (tilt your body and move in an arc), go over a bridge (step high), stop for obstacles on the track (*moo* like cows), pick up cargo (make sloshing noises to mimic liquid-filled barrels). Describe, and encourage children to describe their actions. Use a variety of sounds and movements to represent the train, the terrain it crosses, and the passengers or cargo it picks up. At the end of the activity, slow the train down as it pulls back into the station and the passengers disembark.

Vocabulary words: conductor, exit, journey, on board, passengers, station

Follow-up Ideas

Read books about trains. Once the story is familiar, encourage children to move and make train noises. Bring in photos and paintings of trains. If you live near a train station, arrange a field trip to see the train pull into the station, load passengers or cargo, and depart. Repeat this activity with other multiuse vehicles (e.g., trucks, ships, airplanes). Take an imaginary journey on vehicles children typically ride in or on, such as a car or bicycle. Provide art materials for the children to represent the vehicles, the terrain, passengers and cargo, and adventures en route.

55 Hiccupitis

Content area:
Creative Arts:
Pretend Play

Time of day:
Small-group time

Materials
For each child and teacher: Doll or stuffed animal

To share: Strips of cotton cloth, tape, adhesive bandages, eyedropper, real or toy medical supplies (e.g., stethoscope, thermometer, syringe, latex gloves), paper towels, blankets

For backup: Other props you've observed children use when they play doctor, hospital, or being sick

What Children Do and Learn
Children act out a familiar anxiety-provoking experience such as going to the doctor.

Story Starter
Baby Bear hiccupped all day long. Make hiccupping sounds and jerky movements. *Mama and Papa Bear were worried. "Maybe if we rub some medicine on Baby Bear's chest it will help," they said.* Rub your chest and encourage children to do the same. *But Baby Bear kept hiccupping.* Encourage the children to hiccup with you. *So they went to the doctor. After examining Baby Bear, the doctor said, "This baby has hiccupitis. But I know how to cure it."* Solicit children's ideas on how to cure hiccupitis. Distribute the materials, and say *These babies are sick too. I wonder what's wrong with them and how you'll heal them.*

To scaffold children's vocabulary learning, adults can encourage them to describe and name the babies' symptoms and illnesses, and the medical instruments they are using to examine and treat their "patients."

Scaffolding Children's Learning

Encourage children to describe and name what is wrong with their babies. Say, for example, *I wonder what sickness your baby has. What are your baby's symptoms?* Use gestures and sound effects, and encourage the children to enact the illness in various ways. Repeat and accept the names they give to symptoms and illnesses, including made-up words, and add new words. Describe and name the medical instruments and supplies children use and the ways in which they use them (e.g., *You're putting the thermometer in teddy's mouth to see if he has a fever. I wonder what his temperature is*). Express sympathy and concern for sick babies, and acknowledge when children say they have made a baby better again.

Vocabulary words: *chest, cure, examine, heal, hiccup, medicine, rub*

Follow-up Ideas

At another small-group time, provide art materials for children to represent being sick and going to the doctor or hospital. Read related books such as *Curious George Goes to the Hospital* by H. A. and Margret Rey. Act out other events you've heard the children express concern about, such as the arrival of a new baby, going to kindergarten, parental separation or divorce, the loss of a pet, and so on. Encourage children to use materials and make props to enact these events at work (choice) time. Encourage and support children if they choose to talk about their feelings and how they and their family members cope with them.

56 Hockeyballgolf

Content area:
Creative Arts: Pretend Play

Time of day:
Small-group time

Materials
For each child and teacher: 2–3 safe objects for throwing (e.g., cloth balls, foam balls, rubber balls, wadded-up newspapers wrapped with tape, small basketballs, beanbags)

To share: Large (wide-mouthed) containers such as baskets, buckets, cardboard boxes; pieces of netting; things for hitting the balls (e.g., foam bats, wooden dowels, long-handled spoons, ladles)

For backup: Additional balls, things to hit them with, and containers; whistle, buzzer, bell

What Children Do and Learn
Children invent a new sports game by combining equipment in different ways, making up rules, and creating descriptive names for their games.

Story Starter
Coach Buzzer welcomed the players to the new sports team. "This sport is like nothing you've seen before," the coach said. "It's called hockeyballgolf because it's a hodgepodge of hockey, basketball, and golf." (Invent a name based on two or three sports of interest to children and families in your community.) Talk about the name of the game and children's experiences with various sports. *This sport was so new, no one was quite sure how to play it. Should they throw balls into a basket? Or turn a basket sideways and hit balls into it with a stick? Or toss balls into a net?* Demonstrate a few options and encourage children to imitate and come up with other actions. Distribute the materials and say *Let's see how you use this equipment to play your game.*

Scaffolding Children's Learning
Encourage children to explore the materials and combine them in different ways. Describe, and encourage them to describe, their actions. Repeat the names they give to the equipment, and provide additional labels. Wonder where the coach's name came from; talk about buzzers, whistles, and other signals used at sports events. Invite the children to make up other names for their game and to describe the rules for play. Ask how the games they invent are similar to or different from other sports they know about. Accept that some children may just want to play with the equipment without describing it as a game. Other children may want to collaborate and form "teams" for their games. Support and encourage all these options.

Vocabulary words: buzzer, coach, equipment, hodgepodge, players, sport, team

Follow-up Ideas

Ask children where to store the equipment should they want to play the games they invent at work (choice) time. Bring the equipment outside. Provide children with writing tools if they want to keep score, and ask them to explain their scoring rules. (These rules may be vague and changeable.) Encourage children to make props (e.g., face masks, helmets, numbers to tape to their shirts). Use the equipment to plan (or recall) by having children describe and act out a game (e.g., roll a ball in a container labeled with an area sign) before saying what they will do (or did) at work (choice) time. Ask families to donate unused sports equipment and uniforms. Invite parents to play the games children invent (without winners and losers) at outside time or at school gatherings.

57 Let's Sparkle

Content area:
Creative Arts:
Pretend Play

Time of day:
Small-group time

Materials
For each child and teacher: None

To share: Brightly colored pipe cleaners, ribbons, paper foil, twist ties, rubber bands, shoelaces, beads, metal and color-coated paper clips in different sizes, feathers, glue

For backup: Additional jewelry-making materials such as strips of colored paper, sequins, glue

What Children Do and Learn

Children create and describe jewelry they will wear to a fancy ball to celebrate a town's 100th birthday.

Story Starter

The king and queen of Sparkleville threw a gala party. Why do you think the place where they lived was called Sparkleville? Discuss the children's ideas. *Everyone was invited to the party, and they wore their most sparkly jewelry. The king wore a gold crown on his head and the queen wore a silver tiara on hers.* Talk about what a crown and a tiara are. *Other people put on rings, earrings, necklaces, and watches. What other jewelry do you suppose they wore?* Talk with the children about different kinds of jewelry. Show them the materials, and say *We're invited too. Let's see what kinds of sparkly jewelry we'll make to wear to the gala party.*

Scaffolding Children's Learning

Describe and discuss the jewelry children make, including its characteristics (e.g., color, size, texture, brightness), how they combine and attach materials, and where and how on their bodies they wear the jewelry. If children explore the materials instead of making jewelry, talk about the characteristics of their choices and actions (e.g., bending, wrapping). Label and invite children to label their jewelry. Accept the names they create. Encourage children's problem-solving as they adjust sizes, attach things, and so on.

Put a variety of jewelry-making materials, along with costume jewelry, in the art area, and encourage families to donate items from home.

Vocabulary words: *crown, gala, gold, jewelry, silver, sparkly, tiara*

Follow-up Ideas

Put jewelry-making materials in the art area, and encourage children to think of other items they could use to make jewelry. Make costume jewelry available in the house area, inviting families to donate unused items from home. [Note: check them for safety first.] Bring in advertisements, brochures, and other printed materials featuring jewelry; include items for men as well as women. Encourage children to make jewelry that a character in a familiar story or song might wear.

58 Max and Mona at the Movies

Content area:
Creative Arts: Pretend Play

Time of day:
Small-group time

Materials
For each child and teacher: 2 small figures (e.g., people, animals); top of a small box (or other flat container, approximately 6"–12" per side); 4–5 small- and medium-size blocks as props

To share: Additional props such as figures (to represent the audience), blocks (for ticket booth, concession stand, seats); small pieces of paper (for tickets, popcorn); large sheets of paper (for movie screen)

For backup: Paper and drawing materials (if children want to create other props)

What Children Do and Learn
Children use small figures and other props to act out what to do at the movies.

Story Starter
Max and Mona went to the movie theater. Max started to go inside but Mona said, "We have to buy tickets first." "Where do we do that?" asked Max. Solicit children's ideas. Place a small block in the box and put the figures next to it. *They bought tickets at the ticket booth.* Give each figure a piece of paper. *Mona said, "Let's get popcorn!" Silly Max tried to buy popcorn at the ticket booth.* Ask children what prop to use as popcorn. *Then Max sat on the floor.* Move one figure to the other end of the box. *"You have to sit in a seat!" said Mona.* Put the two figures on small blocks (seats). *"Do we have to push a button for the movie to start?" asked Max.* Distribute the materials and say *Can you help Mona show Max what you do at the movies?*

Scaffolding Children's Learning
Children may re-enact the story you told or change characters and incidents based on their own experiences and imagination. Support and encourage all the ways they use the materials and act out events. Comment on the figures, props, and actions they use (e.g., *You added more seats for the audience; Justin said we should turn out the lights because it's dark inside the movie theater*). Ask children to talk about their experiences of going to the movies with their families, including details about the characters and storyline of the movies they saw, how the theater looked, smelled, and sounded, and other events surrounding the outing.

Vocabulary words: buy, movie, popcorn, screen, theater, ticket

Follow-up Ideas
Bring in ads, posters, and other materials from popular movies the children are familiar with (i.e., those they talk about in class and whose characters they take on during role-play). Ask families to bring in ticket stubs to support the children's role play. Arrange a field trip to a local movie theater (when it's closed) so the children can see the marquee, ticket booth, seats, screen, projection room, concession stand, and so on. Provide dress-up clothes and props for them to re-enact and expand on the characters and plots of movies they see.

Where the Wet Things Are

59

What Children Do and Learn
Children act out characters and events from a familiar book with one signifi-cant element changed (e.g., "wet" instead of "wild" in *Where the Wild Things Are* by Maurice Sendak).

Content area:
Creative Arts:
Pretend Play

Time of day:
Large-group time

Materials
For each child and teacher: None

To share: Where the Wild Things Are by Maurice Sendak (or another book familiar to the children)

For backup: None

Story Starter
Hold up the book *Where the Wild Things Are* and say *Remember what happens when Max goes where the wild things are?* Talk with children about the book, focusing on how the wild things look and move and sound. *One day, Max put on his* wet *suit instead of his wolf suit. He dripped water all over the floor and his mother got angry and called him "wet thing!"* Solicit children's ideas about what else Max did when he wore his wet suit. *Instead of going where the wild things are, Max went to where the* wet *things are. All the monsters squished as they walked* (walk and make squishing noises), *and water dripped down their hairy arms* (pretend to brush water off your arms). *Let's pretend we're monsters where the wet things are too.*

Scaffolding Children's Learning
Encourage children to imagine and act out how wet monsters look, move, and sound. Ask questions such as, *How do wet things dance? How would a Papa (Mama, Baby) wet thing move its arms? What/how does it eat? What do wet things say?* Imitate children. Those who are interested can take turns acting out a wet monster for others to imitate. Encourage children to describe the appearance and actions of the "wet things." Accept that some children will chose to repeat characters and events from the book, rather than act "wet." Or they may just enjoy moving in different ways or making monster noises. Support all their words and actions.

Vocabulary words: drip, hairy, instead, squish, suit, wet

Follow-up Ideas
At small-group time, provide 2-D and 3-D art materials for children to represent how "wet things" look and act. At another large- or small-group time, ask the children to suggest a different type of suit for Max to put on and a place to visit (e.g., small things, soft things, round things). Apply this idea to other books the children are familiar with, that is, change a central character or event, and encourage the children to describe and act out the result. Add props to support their imaginative and pretend play.

Pretend Play

133

60 Who Wants Cake?

Content area:
Creative Arts:
Pretend Play

Time of day:
Large-group time

Materials
*For each child and
teacher:* None

To share: None

For backup: Props
such as plates,
bowls, spoons,
ice cream scoop,
napkins, towels

What Children Do and Learn
Children act out through words, gestures, and movements, how guests of various ages might request cake and ice cream at a birthday party.

Story Starter
Baby Yummy had a birthday party when she was one year old. People of all ages — old and young and in the middle — came to the party. They were hungry! The baby couldn't talk so she pointed to the cake and opened her mouth. Her two-year-old brother said loudly, "Cake! Cake!" Mime eating cake and encourage children to imitate you. *Her mommy put out both hands and said, "Cake and ice cream, please."* Extend your hands, palm up. *Grandpa had a sore throat and couldn't talk, but he wanted ice cream to make his throat feel better. What could he do?* Act out their ideas, and say *Do you want cake and ice cream?*

Scaffolding Children's Learning
Encourage children to take turns and imitate one another as they pretend to ask for and eat cake and ice cream. Ask what else was served at the party. Invite children to think of other older and younger guests, and to act out how they might ask for and eat the food. Make comments to encourage them to represent age or other attributes with language, gestures, and movement (e.g., *How did the old monster show he wanted a big piece of cake? How can your baby chick ask for a piece of candy? If the snake has no hands and can't talk, how do you know what it wants?*). Offer props for children to elaborate on their words and gestures.

Vocabulary words: *age, guest, old, sore throat, young, yummy*

Follow-up Ideas
At work (choice) time, encourage children to describe and represent in words, gestures, and movement, the ages and other attributes of the roles they play. Guess how old the characters are and ask them if and why you are (not) right. When you read books or tell stories, talk and gesture in ways consistent with the characters' ages and other attributes. Encourage children to talk, gesture, and move like people they know of different ages in their families, school, and community. When they invite you to join their role play, ask them to describe how you should act, including what you should say and how you should move.

10

Music

The story starters in Music will involve children in the following learning activities:

- *Exploring sounds* — Listening to, describing, imitating, creating, and comparing sounds

- *Listening and moving to music* — Exploring beat and rhythm, expressing ideas and feelings with music

- *Making music* — Exploring various noise-makers and playing simple instruments

- *Singing* — Exploring vocal qualities, singing and making up songs

- *Music vocabulary* — Learning the terms used to describe musical qualities (tempo, loudness, pitch)

- *Music appreciation* — Exploring musical styles and genres, learning a language to talk about music

61 Attention-Getters

Content area:
Creative Arts: Music

Time of day:
Small-group time

Materials
For each child and teacher: Plastic container with a tight lid; 2–3 sets of small objects used as "fillers" to make different levels of noise when shaken, ranging from little or no noise (e.g., squares of paper, erasers, straw, grass) to moderate noise (e.g., paper clips, dried pasta or beans, shells, gravel, wooden pegs) to loud noise (e.g., nuts and bolts, screws, bells, rocks)

To share: Additional fillers; containers made of other materials (e.g., paper bags, tins, cardboard boxes)

For backup: 2–3 baskets; chart paper divided into two columns (e.g., quiet and loud) or three columns (e.g., quiet, medium, and loud) and markers; baskets

What Children Do and Learn
Children explore the sounds made by collections of small objects in sealed containers to decide if they are loud enough to get the attention of noisy animals.

Story Starter
The zookeeper had a very important announcement to make to all the animals. What do you suppose the zookeeper's message was? Briefly discuss the children's ideas. *The zookeeper wanted to announce that Mr. and Mrs. Panda had a new baby* (or use one of the children's ideas). *But the owls kept hooting, the lions kept roaring, and the snakes kept hissing until the zookeeper got frustrated trying to get their attention. He decided to make a noisemaker louder than the animals to get their attention and make his announcement.* Put materials that make very little noise (e.g., grass clippings) in the container, shake it, and ask *Do you think this will work?* Try another type of filler (e.g., pea gravel), and ask *How about this?* Give each child a container and a set of fillers, and say *Let's make attention-getters so the zookeeper can announce his important message to the animals.*

Scaffolding Children's Learning
Encourage children to explore, predict, and describe the loudness of filler materials. Pose challenges (e.g., *Would I use paper clips or rocks if the horses were neighing really loudly?*). Midway through the activity, introduce containers made of different materials and encourage children to compare how they affect the level of sound. If children are interested, set out baskets so they can sort materials, or make a chart comparing two or three categories of loudness.

Vocabulary words: announcement, attention, louder, noiseless, noisemaker, quieter

Follow-up Ideas
Make a book with pictures of quiet, medium, and loud noisemakers; encourage children to add pictures as they make more observations and discoveries about different noises and sounds. Make attention-getters of varying levels of loudness to alert children to transitions. Ask children to predict which noise levels will be most effective, and discuss which ones work and why. Use attention-getters to help children take turns as leader at large-group time (e.g., a child passes it to the next leader who shakes it before making his or her suggestion to the group). Solicit children's ideas at other times during the daily routine when you or they might use attention-getters to encourage members of the class to listen to one another.

Bee and Bop Birthday Party

62

What Children Do and Learn
Children listen to, describe, and dance to fast and slow musical selections.

Story Starter
The Bee and Bop twins invited all their friends to a dance party to celebrate their birthday. Bop liked fast, lively music you could bounce to, but Bee liked slow, gentle music you could sway to. Encourage the children to "bounce" and then to "sway." *To solve the problem, Bee and Bop played both kinds of music at their party — some to bounce to and some to sway to. Let's listen to the music and dance along with them.* Play a selection, let children listen, ask if they think it is fast or slow, and dance for a minute. Then say *It's time to change the music.* Put on a different tempo, let the children listen, describe the music, and begin to dance.

Scaffolding Children's Learning
Play fast and slow music in random order, encouraging children to listen and name the tempo (fast or slow) before they begin dancing. Describe, and encourage them to describe how they move. Say *I wonder what other ways we can move to this music.* Discuss how different musical qualities elicit different movements (e.g., *Rhonda skipped to the bouncy tune. Now*

Content area:
Creative Arts: Music

Time of day:
Large-group time

Materials
For each child and teacher: None

To share: Music player and instrumental music selections with fast (e.g., lively, bouncy) and slow (e.g., swaying, swinging) tempos, played in random order (i.e., not regular alternation), each lasting 1–2 minutes

For backup:
Objects to hold while dancing (e.g., scarves, paper plates)

In this activity, teachers play several selections of fast and slow music as children listen to and name the tempo before they begin dancing.

she's gliding to the slow, steady sound of this melody). After several selections, ask children to predict what they think will be next and to verify their prediction after the music starts. Offer objects for children to hold and move with as they dance.

Vocabulary words: *bounce, fast, gentle, lively, slow, sway, music*

Follow-up Ideas

For transitions, play a piece of music and encourage children to move to the next activity according to how the music makes them feel. Describe the music and their accompanying movements. When children choose songs to sing (e.g., from the class song book), ask whether they think the song is fast or slow, happy or sad, lively or quiet, and so on. Make a chart and tally how many of each type there are in the song book.

Bingo's Babies

63

What Children Do and Learn
Children sing alternative rhyming names for a dog in the song "B-I-N-G-O."
(Children should already be familiar with the song.)

Content area:
Creative Arts: Music

Time of day:
Large-group time

Materials
For each child and teacher: None

To share: None

For backup: Chart paper and marker

Story Starter
Remember the song about a farmer and a dog named Bingo? Sing with the children, *"There was a farmer had a dog and* Bingo *was its name-o. B-I-N-G-O, B-I-N-G-O, B-I-N-G-O, and* Bingo *was its name-o." Then Bingo gave birth to puppies and the farmer had to come up with different names to put on their dog collars. The farmer named one puppy* Lingo. *It starts with the /L/ sound.* Sing with the children, *"There was a farmer had another dog and* Lingo *was its name-o. L-I-N-G-O, L-I-N-G-O, L-I-N-G-O, and* Lingo *was its name-o." There were still lots of puppies who needed names. Let's help the farmer think of more names.*

Scaffolding Children's Learning
Encourage the children to think up more names for the puppies. When they suggest a name, emphasize the initial sound and say the new name before singing the song (e.g., *Yoshi named a puppy* Zingo, *with the /Z/ sound. "There was a farmer…"*). Instead of a rhyming name, children may say their own name, a pet's name, or another real or made-up name. Accept their suggestions, repeat the name, and sing it with the children. For a long name or unfamiliar letters, use the first letter (e.g., *"There was a farmer had a dog and* Kendra *was its name-o.* Kendra *starts with the /K/ sound."* [Sing "Kendra *starts with the* K *sound* three times"] and finish with "*and* Kendra *was its name-o*"). If children are interested, write, or have them write, the first letter of the name they suggest on the chart paper.

To follow up on this activity, teachers can have children choose a song from the class song book at large-group time and decide on the words they want to substitute.

Vocabulary words: another, birth, dog collar, farmer, puppies

Follow-up Ideas

At planning, recall, and transition times, substitute children's names or attributes in familiar songs. For example, at recall, using the tune of "Did You Ever See a Lassie?" sing *Isaac went to work time, to work time, to work time, Isaac went to work time and played with the ____* (child fills in something he or she played with). When getting ready for outside time, alter the words to "Twinkle, Twinkle, Little Star," singing instead *Twinkle, twinkle, all the blue shoes, it's your turn to get your coat.* At large-group time, have children choose a song from the class song book and say which word(s) in the song they want the class to take turns substituting. Write down their ideas and store them with the song book for children to use on their own at work (choice) time.

Bird Choir

64

What Children Do and Learn
Children sing a familiar song in different ways to explore vocal variations in pitch, tempo, and volume.

Content area:
Creative Arts: Music

Time of day:
Large-group time

Materials
For each child and teacher: None

To share: Class song book

For backup: None

Story Starter
The birds felt sad and unappreciated. The other animals in the forest thought all birds sounded alike. The birds wanted them to know that birds make many different kinds of sounds. So the birds formed a choir to showcase their differences. Have you ever heard a choir? Discuss the children's experiences and say *A choir is a group of singers whose voices range from low* (sing a low note) *to medium* (demonstrate and encourage the children to join in) *to high* (sing a high note with the children). *The birds picked out a song from the Flock Song Book* (open the class song book and choose a favorite song). *The bass birds sang it very low* (demonstrate and encourage the children to join in a verse or chorus). *The alto and tenor birds sang mid-pitch, and the soprano birds sang very high* (sing a line or verse at each pitch with the children.) *The other forest animals asked the bird choir to sing more songs. Let's pick another song and sing this one in a high, medium, and low voice.*

Scaffolding Children's Learning
Encourage children who want to pick a song and choose the pitch(es) at which to sing it. Repeat children's suggestions so everyone can hear, then help them begin to sing the song at that pitch. Midway through the activity, say *The bird choir wanted the other animals to know that they could also sing at different speeds or tempos. Let's sing the next song really slow.* Then sing the same song at a faster tempo. After singing two or three songs that vary in tempo, encourage the children to sing a song at different levels of loudness. Encourage them to label and compare variations in pitch, tempo, and volume. [For younger children, or earlier in the year, you might stay with pitch for the entire activity. Introduce the other dimensions — tempo and/or loudness — at subsequent group times.] Talk about the children's experiences listening to live and recorded vocal groups at religious services, concerts, on the radio, and so on. Ask if their family members sing in a vocal group such as a glee club or barbershop quartet.

Vocabulary words: *alike, alto, bass, choir, flock, pitch, soprano, tempo, tenor, unappreciated, volume*

Follow-up Ideas
Play the song by folk singer Bill Staines called "A Place in the Choir." Listen to chorale music with distinctive vocal ranges. Sing a song or recite a chant using a different pitch. Ask children to suggest another pitch and/or use the same pitch with a different song. Ask how a familiar character in a story might say or sing something (e.g., *How do you think the Papa Bear would sing the Eensy Weensy Spider? What about Mama Bear? Baby Bear?*). Repeat this activity but instead of varying pitch, change the speed (tempo) or loudness of the song.

Earlings

65

What Children Do and Learn
Children make sounds characteristic of different objects.

Story Starter
Creatures called Earlings landed on Earth. Why do you think they were called Earlings? Ask for the children's ideas. *They were called Earlings because they had very big ears.* Have children show with their hands how big they think their ears were. *The Earlings were very curious about sounds. Whenever they found something, they asked, "What does this sound like?"* Point to an object (e.g., toy fire engine), encourage the children make its sound, and imitate them. Repeat with another object (e.g., toy animal). Give each child an object, point to the other objects, and say *Let's help the Earlings learn what sounds these things make.*

Scaffolding Children's Learning
Encourage children to make the sounds characteristic of different objects. Supply object names and noises when asked, and refer children to one another for help. If children play with objects without making sounds, imitate their actions and supply sounds in your own play. Do not correct

Content area:
Creative Arts: Music

Time of day:
Small-group time

Materials
For each child and teacher: Object that is associated with a distinctive sound but that does not itself make the sound (e.g., animal figure such as a cat or dog, toy train or fire engine without a bell, tea kettle, nonworking clock)

To share: Additional objects identified with sound (e.g., telephone, frying pan)

For backup: Objects that do not make distinctive or obvious sounds (e.g., book, paper, plastic bowl)

Encourage children to listen to and identify sounds in the classroom and in the outdoor environment.

errors, but you might say, *When I use my stapler, it goes* click, click *every time I press the handle.* Make the sound of an object for children to guess; ask them to make a sound for you to guess. Midway through the activity, if children appear ready, say *Here are some tricky ones,* and introduce objects that make no sound or very subtle sounds.

Vocabulary words: *buzz, clang, curious, ear(s), sound, whoosh*

Follow-up Ideas

Create "sound cards" with pictures of things that do and do not make sounds for children to sort at another small-group time. Make two books for the class library labeled "Sounds" and "Silence," and encourage children to add magazine pictures or their own drawings. Play sound guessing games (e.g., *I'm thinking of something in the toy area that makes a noise like* pop, pop, pop. *What do you think it is?*). Record sounds in the classroom and outdoors, and encourage children to listen and guess what they are. Give sound clues at message board time (e.g., *There's something new in the toy area and it makes a* whirr *sound. What do you think it is?*).

Fairy Ball

66

What Children Do and Learn

Children use scarves and streamers to move to music in different genres and from different cultures.

Story Starter

Fairies from all over the world gathered for the fairy ball. Ask children what they think the words *fairy ball* mean in this story, then explain: *A ball is a big dance party where everyone gets dressed up and dances to different kinds of music. Each girl and boy fairy at the ball brought the kind of music they listened to at home. Because fairies fly, they brought scarves that flew through the air with them when they danced.* Play and label one selection (e.g., *This is a string quartet. The music is played by two violins, a viola, and a cello. Let's listen*). After 5–10 seconds, say *It's time for the fairies and their scarves to dance.*

Children can make their own streamers — and take them outside — to use as props while dancing to different types and styles of music.

Scaffolding Children's Learning

After children dance for a while, play another kind of music brought by a different fairy. Say what it is (e.g., *drums from Brazil*), and encourage children to listen briefly (some will continue to move) and dance in whatever way the music makes them feel. Play and label music from another genre, either one that children may have heard at home (e.g., salsa, jazz, reggae) or one that is unfamiliar (throat chanting, yodeling). Dance with the children and comment on your actions (e.g., *This violin music is slow and dreamy. I'm gliding and fluttering my scarves behind me*). Encourage children to describe the music and their movements.

Content area:
Creative Arts: Music

Time of day:
Large-group time

Materials
For each child and teacher: 2 scarves or streamers (e.g., made of crepe paper or nylon)

To share: Music player and instrumental music selections in 3–4 different genres and with a variety of instruments and sounds (e.g., classical, jazz, swing, folk, different tonal scales, percussion, strings, woodwinds, shape-note singing); include music representative of children's cultures, as well as styles they may never have heard before

For backup: Other lightweight props to hold while dancing (e.g., feathers, paper plates, ribbon, ribbon rings, braided yarn, fabric strips)

Vocabulary words: ball, fairy, flutter, jazz, quartet, string, yodel

Follow-up Ideas

Repeat this activity throughout the year, each time playing familiar styles while gradually introducing new ones. Provide materials in the art area for children to make their own streamers. Bring streamers outdoors if children want to move with them at outside time. Play or sing different types of music at transitions, and encourage children to move to the next activity based on how the music makes them feel. Encourage families to loan CDs of the types of music played at home. Invite family members who play music to visit and play for the children. Invite performers who specialize in playing for children to visit the classroom. Take the class — and encourage families to go — to concerts geared for children.

Musical Jamboree

67

What Children Do and Learn
Children act out what they like to do when they listen to different genres of music.

Content area:
Creative Arts: Music

Time of day:
Large-group time

Materials
For each child and teacher: None

To share: Music player and music selections in 3–4 different genres and styles, reflecting the diversity and interests of families in the program (e.g., classical, jazz, blues, gospel, rock, dance, rap, country, western swing, Zydeco, drum or other percussion solos, banjo or guitar picking, scales, folk, and world music from different continents and countries)

For backup: None

Story Starter
A group of children had a Musical Jamboree. They each brought a different kind of music and said what they did whenever they played it. Play and label one selection, describe what you like to do, and encourage the children to imitate you (e.g., *This is a symphony. When I hear a symphony, I pretend to conduct the orchestra*). Mime conducting with your arms and encourage children to copy you. Play another selection (e.g., *This is a waltz. When my friend plays a waltz, he likes to sweep the floor*). Demonstrate and encourage the children to sweep to waltz music. Say *I wonder what you like to do when you hear different kinds of music.*

Scaffolding Children's Learning
Label and encourage children to label the music. Do not correct them, but provide additional labels (e.g., *Natalie calls this plinky-plunky music. Sometimes I also call it banjo music*). Encourage them to say and demonstrate what they like to do to each type of music. If they simply move to the music, describe their movement and encourage others to imitate it. If they name something they like without moving, ask them to describe the movements they would use (e.g., *How should we move to show we're painting the wall?*). For children who move on their own, describe and imitate their movements (e.g., *Josh, I'm sliding to the music just like you*).

Vocabulary words: *conduct, genre, jamboree, orchestra, symphony, waltz*

Follow-up Ideas
Repeat this activity with other musical genres throughout the year. Encourage families to bring in music they play at home. Ask families when they play music at home and what they do while listening; share this background with the children. Play different types of music at transitions, and encourage children to perform an action that fits the music as they move to the next activity. Once children are familiar with different genres, ask them what type of music to play during specific activities (e.g., *What kind of music should we play while we clean up?*).

68 Musical Squares

Content area:
Creative Arts: Music

Time of day:
Large-group time

Materials
For each child and teacher:
Carpet or fabric squares arranged in a circle (several more squares than people)

To share: Music player and instrumental music selection(s)

For backup: None

What Children Do and Learn

In a variation on musical chairs, children listen to music, move around squares in different ways, stand on a square when the music stops, and perform a simple action.

Story Starter

A place called Musical Squares *was unusual in two ways. First, instead of using clocks to know when it was time to do something, they listened to music. When the music stopped, it was time to do something like eat breakfast, brush your teeth, or go to school. Second, people in Musical Squares didn't sit in chairs. They stood on ___* (pause for children to fill in the word) *squares to do everything. When the music stopped, they stood on squares to do things and even slept standing up on squares! Let's try it, brushing our teeth when the music stops.* Start the music, walk with children around the squares, stop the music, and say *Time to stand on a square and brush our teeth.* Stop and pantomime brushing your teeth with the children.

Scaffolding Children's Learning

Start the music again, stop it, and suggest another activity (e.g., driving to school). Keep the activity going, stopping only briefly before restarting the music. Once children have the idea, have them take turns suggesting what to do on the square when the music stops. Midway through the activity, ask children to suggest ways other than walking to move around the squares (e.g., skip, crawl, gallop, stomp, or tip-toe). If children seem confused about when to stop or what to do, say something like *I'm watching Fariyal* (name a child who understands the activity) *and copying what she does. Fariyal, is it okay if Bethany copies you too?*

Vocabulary words: *clock, musical, pantomime, square, start, stop*

Follow-up Ideas

Adapt this activity to play Musical Areas at planning or recall time. Put area signs in a circle on the floor, play and stop the music, and have children stand on the area they plan to play in or did play in at work (choice) time. Make sure there are enough signs of each area so several children can find one to stand on. Play Musical Numbers, labeling squares of paper with numerals (begin with 1–3), or cut out Musical Shapes. When the music stops, suggest activities based on the number or shape (e.g., *Clap the same number of times as the numeral you're standing on; If you're on a circle, wiggle your foot. If you're on a square, wave your hand*).

Old Songs, New Words

What Children Do and Learn
Children substitute words in a familiar song as they keep the melody constant but make up different lyrics.

Content area:
Creative Arts: Music

Time of day:
Large-group time

Materials
For each child and teacher: None

To share: Class song book

For backup: None

Story Starter
Missy McBride loved to sing. She sang on her way to school and in the bathtub. Her favorite song was "The Farmer in the Dell." But there was a problem. Missy McBride could never remember the words to the song. She knew the tune but the words flew right out of her head! So she made up her own lyrics. On her way to school, she sang, "The teacher in the school, the teacher in the school, hi ho the derry-o, the teacher in the school." Sing it twice through with the children. *In the bathtub, she sang, "The girl in the tub, the girl in the tub, hi ho the derry-o, the girl in the tub."* Sing it together twice and say *What other verses can we make up*?

Scaffolding Children's Learning
Encourage children to contribute their ideas, and sing each idea at least twice through before turning to the next child. Some children may choose to sing the actual words, some will repeat the lyrics from your story or another child's suggestion, and some may contribute original ideas. Whatever their suggestions, accept and sing them. If necessary, clarify and repeat a child's idea to make sure everyone understands it. Midway through the activity, ask the children to suggest another song from memory or the class song book. Talk with them about the parts of a song, that is, the melody (tune) and the words (e.g., lyrics, verse, or chorus).

Vocabulary words: *chorus, lyrics, melody, substitute, tune, verse*

Follow-up Ideas
Sing other familiar songs, substituting words to fit the situation. For example, at cleanup time, to the tune of "Row, Row, Row Your Boat," sing "Put, put, put away the toys." During work (choice) or outside time, sing what children are doing (e.g., to "Twinkle, Twinkle Little Star," sing *"John is painting with red paint, Emily is using blue"*). Once children get the idea, encourage them to sing their plans or recall their work (choice) time activities to a familiar melody. For example, to the tune of "Did You Ever See a Lassie?" you can sing, *"What will you do at work time, at work time, at work time?"* and the child can sing, *"I'm going to the house area."*

70 Pat a Pizza

Content area:
Creative Arts: Music

Time of day:
Large-group time

Materials
For each child and teacher: None

To share: None

For backup: Letters (e.g., wood, plastic, foam, cardboard)

What Children Do and Learn
Singing and patting to the nursery rhyme "Pat a Cake," children substitute the names of other foods in place of cake.

Story Starter
Do you know the song, "Pat a Cake"? Sing and pat the beat on your knees with the children: *"Pat a cake, pat a cake, baker's man. Make me a cake as fast as you can. Roll it, and pinch it and mark it with a B, and put it in the oven for Baby and me."* The pizza man heard the baker singing and liked the song so much, he made up his own song about pizza. He called it *"Pat a Pizza."* Let's sing it together. *"Pat a pizza, pat a pizza, pizza man…"* Sing and pat the song with the children. Ask what foods they like to eat and say *How can we sing the song using the word* ____ (whatever foods they name)? Half the time, substitute baker's *woman* for baker's *man*.

Using the familiar "Pat a Cake" chant, children are encouraged to substitute the names of different foods and "pat" the beat as they sing the melody.

Scaffolding Children's Learning

Encourage children to suggest foods and lead the group in singing. They may choose to sing the original song, repeat foods named by others, or suggest new ones. Some children may pat without singing, or vice versa. Acknowledge and support whatever they do (e.g., *Aaron, you're patting to the yogurt woman*). Emphasize and pat the beat even when children suggest multisyllable words by saying the words quickly to fall on the beat (e.g., spa-*ghet*-ti man). Midway through the activity, ask children to suggest another place to pat. Depending on their developmental level, children may suggest one or more other substitutions. For example, they may suggest a letter other than *B,* such as the initial of their first name, and choose to hold and pat their body with that letter (using backup materials). They may also substitute a different word for oven (e.g., the refrigerator).

Vocabulary words: *baker, food, pat the beat, pizza, steady beat*

Follow-up Ideas

Add "Pat a Cake" to the class song book. Use this rhyme to sing and pat at planning or recall time (e.g., "*Samuel, Samuel, tell us your plan*"; "*Darla, Darla, where did you work?*"). Children can also choose a relevant object to tap on the table such as a block, puzzle piece, or paintbrush (i.e., for the block, toy, or art area, respectively). They may want to tap with the letter that begins their name. If children are interested, encourage them to add letters to the foods they create with play dough or other materials in the house area.

71 Ridiculous Rock Band

Content area:
Creative Arts: Music

Time of day:
Large-group time

Materials
For each child and teacher: None

To share: Things that can represent instruments but do not themselves make noise (e.g., blocks children can strum like guitars, shake like maracas, blow at one end like woodwinds or brass; pieces of cardboard they can plunk like pianos or tap like xylophones; funnels they can toot or tap together; paper plates they can hit like drums or knock together like cymbals; chopsticks they can use as a baton or bow for string instruments)

For backup: None

What Children Do and Learn
Children invent sounds to accompany their actions with nonmusical objects that represent instruments.

Story Starter
The Ridiculous Rock Band was hired to perform at (name a local stadium or park familiar to the children). *Do you know why they were called the Ridiculous Rock Band?* Discuss the children's ideas about the meaning of *ridiculous,* using words such as *silly* or *not acting like other bands.* Say *They got their name because they didn't play real instruments. They used blocks and paper plates* (name and point to several of the shared materials) *and made up their own musical sounds to go with them.* Demonstrate with one item (e.g., strum a block, make a twanging sound to a lively beat). Point to the rest of the items, and say *How do you think the Ridiculous Rock Band sounded when they played music with these?*

As members of a band, children use a variety of materials to represent musical instruments and pretend to make their sounds.

Scaffolding Children's Learning

Encourage the children to explore and "play" the materials, having them switch two or three times so they try a variety. Describe, and encourage children to describe, the volume and other musical qualities of their sounds. Accept their descriptive labels, both real words (e.g., *banjo*) and made-up expressions (e.g., *plunker*). Invite them to name familiar instruments, and provide the names of less familiar instruments. If they mislabel an instrument, do not correct them but say *Sometimes I call that instrument a* _____ (fill in the correct name). If children gesture without making sounds, ask if you or the other children can invent a sound to accompany their movements. Encourage children to listen to and imitate one another's sounds.

Vocabulary words: *band, instrument, musical, perform, sound*

Follow-up Ideas

Listen to recorded music and have children identify which instruments are being played. Provide simple percussion and other instruments for children to explore at work (choice) time and during other small- and large-group activities. Close your eyes and guess what instruments they are playing; have them close their eyes and guess what instrument you are playing. Encourage children to represent these instruments in non-musical ways (e.g., with 2-D and 3-D art materials, or through role play with their voices and gestures).

72   Tap Town

Content area:
Creative Arts: Music

Time of day:
Large-group time

Materials
For each child and teacher: None

To share: Music player and instrumental recording (or teacher's voice) of a familiar tune with a steady beat

For backup: None

What Children Do and Learn

Children tap parts of their bodies as they listen to a familiar tune with a steady beat.

Story Starter

Every morning, the mayor of Tap Town played the song ___ (name a tune with a steady beat that is familiar to the children (e.g., "Alley Cat") on the loudspeaker to wake up the townspeople. When they got up, they'd tap the place on their body that had the same name as the street where they lived. The people on Head Street would tap their heads. Play or hum the tune and tap your heads to the beat as the children imitate you. *Everyone who lived on Knee Street got out of bed and tapped their ___.* Wait for the children to fill in *knees,* then play or hum the tune and tap your knees. *Where do you like to tap when you hear the music?*

Scaffolding Children's Learning

With each repetition, encourage one child to name a street and/or place to tap. Repeat their idea to make sure everyone understands (e.g., *Joshua says the people on Nose Street tapped their noses*). Children may just name a body part, though some may also name a street. They may choose a street or body part already named by others or suggest a new one. Accept and carry out their ideas. If children are unsure about where to tap, say something like *I'm watching Talia to see where she taps* (name a child who knows where to tap). When children are comfortable with the activity, you might ask what other times of day the mayor of Tap Town played music for people to tap to. You might also introduce words other than *street,* such as *avenue* or *road,* using labels commonly found in your area that children have heard or are likely to hear.

Vocabulary words: *lived, loudspeaker, mayor, townspeople, street, tap*

Follow-up Ideas

Play or sing music with a steady beat at transition times and encourage children to walk or march to the beat to the next activity. Tap a steady beat at planning or recall time, and use a familiar chant or song to describe what children will do or did at work (choice) time. For example, to the tune of "Did You Ever See a Lassie?" sing and tap *"George played in the art area, the art area, the art area. George played in the art area and painted with red paint."* Play "Simon Says," using repeated motions to a familiar tune with a steady beat, for example, *Simon Says* march *while I sing "The Farmer in the Dell." Simon says* stop. *Simon says* hop *while I sing "The Farmer in the Dell." Simon says* stop. And so on. Encourage children to suggest forward movements.

At transition times, teachers can play music with a steady beat as children walk or march to the next activity.

11

Physical Development and Health

Story starters in Physical Development and Health will encourage children to learn about:

- *Locomotor and nonlocomotor skills —* Moving in place and moving across space

- *Stability skills —* Balancing

- *Fine- and large-motor manipulative skills —* Using hands, arms, feet, and legs to handle and propel objects

- *Sequencing movements —* Ordering two movements; ordering three or more movements

- *Nutrition —* Eating healthy foods

- *Caring for our bodies —* Practicing self-care routines and learning about food and nutrition

73 Absent-Minded Doctor

Content area:
Physical
Development
and Health

Time of day:
Large-group time

Materials
For each child and teacher: None

To share: None

For backup: None

What Children Do and Learn
Children invent and describe different movements to identify and label parts of their bodies.

Story Starter
Yasmine went to the doctor for a check-up. Talk about children's trips to the doctor. *The doctor looked in Yasmine's ears* (encourage children to tap their ears) *and said, "Your ears are fine. The examination is over. I'll see you again next year." But Yasmine protested, "You haven't checked the rest of my body to see if I'm healthy." The doctor apologized, "I'm sorry. I'm very absent-minded."* Discuss the meaning of *absent-minded* (forgetful). *"Show me what other body parts to examine." Yasmine did this* (pull out your cheeks) *to remind the doctor to look at her ___* (pause for children to say "cheeks" and pull out theirs). *What clues can we give the absent-minded doctor to check other parts of our bodies?*

When children are playing doctor, encourage them to name where on the body the baby is hurt or needs "medicine."

Scaffolding Children's Learning

Encourage the children to take turns indicating body parts with different movements. Describe the movement and have children name the body part (e.g., *Wyatt is bending and tapping his ___ [knee]*). After providing a couple of examples, encourage children to describe their movement as well as name the part (e.g., *Can you tell us where you're jabbing?*). Point to parts of your body as children name them. Now and then, if they give a general response (e.g., leg), ask *Where on your leg should the doctor look?* Supply names the children may not know (e.g., *Sarah is rubbing her* thigh. *That's the part of the leg above the knee*).

Vocabulary words: *absent-minded, body part, check-up, clue, examine, healthy*

Follow-up Ideas

As you play as a partner during children's doll or stuffed-animal play, name body parts when they are relevant to the play theme (e.g., *The baby's forehead feels warm. I think she has a fever*). When children play doctor, encourage them to be specific about what is injured or where it hurts (e.g., *Where on the daddy's arm does it hurt? Is it down at the wrist or up near the shoulder?*). Ask for directions administering "medicine" (e.g., *Where should I give the baby a shot? On which part of her leg?*). When you describe children's movements or read a book, mention the body part involved in the motion (e.g., *The monsters are lifting their knees high in the air*). Encourage children to imitate actions in books and name the body parts involved. Supply additional labels.

74 Anything But Your Car, Car

Content area:
Physical Development and Health

Time of day:
Large-group time

Materials
For each child and teacher: None

To share: None

For backup: Toy vehicles other than cars

What Children Do and Learn
Children use gestures and body movements to represent different types of vehicles. (Children should be familiar with the song "Take Me for a Ride in Your Car, Car.")

Story Starter
You know the song "Take Me for a Ride in Your Car, Car." Sing it once through with the children. *Well, one day all the cars were broken down so the people had to go places using other kinds of vehicles. Some took an airplane* (spread your arms and fly in a small circle), *and when they traveled by plane they sang, "Take me for a ride in your airplane." Others rode a bicycle* (pedal your arms or get on your back and pedal) *and sang, "Take me for a ride on your bicycle." Suppose they traveled by boat? How would they move?* Use the children's movement suggestions and sing, *"Take me for a float on your boat, boat." How else do you think they got around without cars?* Solicit the children's ideas, and choose one of their suggestions to start with.

Scaffolding Children's Learning
Encourage the children to take turns naming vehicles, demonstrating how they move, and saying how to adapt the words of the song. Some children may move on their own without following a leader, some may lead a movement without singing the song, and some may name a vehicle but neither move nor sing. Support whatever children do (e.g., describe their movements, ask if their vehicle has a name, suggest how to sing the song, or ask another child to suggest the words). Offer challenges now and then (e.g., *Some people took a pogo stick. How does a pogo stick move?*). Demonstrate if needed and sing *Take me for a jump on your pogo stick.* Suggest other familiar and less familiar ideas such as a helicopter, motorcycle, ambulance, hay wagon, or snowmobile. Hold up a toy vehicle such as a piece of construction equipment (e.g., *Suppose they traveled in a crane. How does a crane move?*). If children suggest a car, don't correct them. Use and imitate their idea, perhaps with a comment, such as *The mechanic fixed Jessica's car so we can ride in it!*

Vocabulary words: *airplane, broken, mechanic, pogo stick, travel, vehicle*

Follow-up Ideas

Have children move like different types of vehicles at transition times. At planning time, encourage them to drive a vehicle to the area where they will begin work (choice) time. At recall time, have them load an object or material they used at work time into a vehicle and drive it to the recall table. Put books, catalogs, ads, travel brochures, and other printed materials about vehicles (e.g., cars, trucks, trains, planes, boats) in the book area. Read and look at them with the children. Go on a neighborhood walk and talk about the different kinds of vehicles you see. At outside time, pause to listen to and identify vehicles by the sounds they make.

75 Big New Playground

Content area:
Physical Development and Health

Time of day:
Small-group time

Materials
For each child and teacher: 4–5 blocks of different sizes and shapes

To share: Additional blocks, boxes, carpet squares, other building materials

For backup: Pictures of your playground; pictures of other playgrounds varying in size and design

What Children Do and Learn
Children build a large, multipart structure with blocks and other materials, working alone or collaborating in pairs and small groups.

Story Starter
So many new children came to preschool that there wasn't enough playground equipment for everyone to use outside. So the teachers and families all got together to build new playground equipment. One parent said, "Let's make a tower so children can climb up and see over the rooftops!" Stack some blocks in a tower and encourage children to do the same. *A child said, "I like to draw outside. Let's make a table and chairs where children can draw."* Build a simple table. Talk to the children about what they like to do at outside time, distribute the materials, and say *I wonder what equipment you will build on your playground.*

As a follow-up to this activity, teachers can make up a story about another large structure for the children to build, encouraging them to draw plans before they start building.

Scaffolding Children's Learning

Encourage children to spread out on the table and surrounding floor area; extend into other classroom areas if it does not interfere with another group's small-group activity. Remind children they can work alone, in pairs, or in small groups. Circulate around the room as they build. Comment on and describe the materials they use, especially noting their actions with them (e.g., *Sofia is lifting another block to the top of the tower; You're making a wide path across the mud field*). Ask children to demonstrate the movements (e.g., sliding, climbing, jumping) they will make when they use the new playground equipment. Encourage children to compare what they build to the pictures of playgrounds.

Vocabulary words: *build, construction, equipment, playground, rooftops, tower*

Follow-up Ideas

Make up a story about another large multipart structure for the children to build, such as a school, shopping center, or apartment complex (i.e., a type of structure they are familiar with). Read books and bring in pictures that show these structures in different sizes and designs. Provide art materials for children to represent their structures. Encourage them to draw plans beforehand and relate what they build to their plans. If children want to continue building a structure over two or more days, provide "work-in-progress" signs. Encourage children to explain their structures and how they built them to their parents. Visit a construction site (following safety procedures) and take photographs. Talk with children about the materials and actions of the construction workers.

76 Construction Zone

Content area:
Physical Development and Health

Time of day: Small-group time

Materials
For each child and teacher:
Lightweight hammers; pounding surfaces (Styrofoam blocks, thick cardboard, planks of soft wood); things to pound (golf tees, nails); safety goggles [Note: Early in the year use golf tees and Styrofoam or cardboard; later in the year use nails and wood.]

To share: Other soft materials to pound things into (e.g., play dough, clay, beeswax)

For backup: Other materials for pounding (e.g., rubber mallets, heavy-duty cardboard tubes)

What Children Do and Learn
Children describe their actions and how their movements are affected as they use hammers to pound with and into different materials.

Story Starter
One day before my alarm clock rang, I was awakened by a loud hammering noise. Ask the children if they have ever been awakened by hammering. *It was my next-door neighbor, building a deck on her house. Since I was awake, I went for an early morning walk. Everywhere I went, more people were pounding with hammers. One person was building a swing set, another was fixing a window, and it looked like someone else was building a rocket ship to the moon! What else do you suppose my neighbors were using their hammers for?* Solicit the children's ideas. *It's fun to fix and build things. But first it's good to practice using a hammer. Let's try these hammers. Maybe we'll get some ideas of things we'd like to build.*

Teachers can describe children's motions with hammers and other tools, and comment on the hardness and softness of materials the children are pounding.

Scaffolding Children's Learning

Make sure children have enough room to swing the hammers freely without hitting one another. Encourage them to explore the materials and use them in different combinations. Describe, and encourage children to describe, their motions (e.g., *Lola is raising her arm high before she pounds down with the hammer*). Capture the rhythm of children's movements by chanting (e.g., *Knock, knock, knock. Down comes the hammer*). Comment on the hardness and softness of the materials they are pounding (e.g., *The Styrofoam feels softer than the wood. I wonder which one it will be easier to pound the nails into*). Help children problem-solve, and encourage them to help one another (e.g., *Maybe Tasha can show you how she got the golf tee to stand upright in the clay*). Comment if they make patterns with the tees or nails. Talk about what they'd like to build.

Vocabulary words: *bang, hammer (noun and verb), knock, pound, raise, swing (verb)*

Follow-up Ideas

Set up a construction area in the classroom with tools, safety goggles, and a flat work space. Ask families to donate scrap wood to the area. Add other tools such as hand drills. Draw the area symbols on a piece of Styrofoam (or cardboard or a wooden block), and have children pound a golf tee or nail into the area where they will (or did) work. Bring the materials outside, and encourage children to add others (e.g., twigs) and to explore hammering things into different surfaces, such as tree stumps, mounds of gravel, or clay-dense soil.

77 Exercise, Exercise

Content area:
Physical
Development
and Health

Time of day:
Large-group time

Materials
For each child and teacher: None

To share: None

For backup:
Scarves, streamers, paper plates, or other objects to move with

What Children Do and Learn
Children create and copy physical exercises that sequence two movements.

Story Starter
Burt and Betty were twins. Explain that twins are two children born at the same time who are exactly the same age. *Because there were two of them, they did everything in pairs.* Pair *is another word for two* (hold up two fingers). *When they ate fruit, they always ate an apple* and *an orange* (point to each finger). *Burt and Betty also liked to exercise. It was fun and helped them stay healthy. They made up a game called "Exercise, Exercise" where they did pairs of different movements. In one pair, they stretched their arms over their heads, and then they bent down to touch their toes.* Demonstrate and encourage children to imitate the two motions. *In another pair, they twisted sideways and then they ___* (solicit children's ideas). *What other "exercise, exercise" can we do?*

Scaffolding Children's Learning
Have children take turns as leaders, suggesting a sequence of two exercises. One child may suggest both movements, or two children can each suggest a movement. Help them describe the movements and demonstrate them for the others to follow. Pose challenges (e.g., *Let's try a pair of exercises where the first is with our arms and the second is with our legs*). Prompt the leader and give all the children cues, such as *What's the first exercise?* After several repeats, say *It's time for the second "exercise, exercise."* Encourage children to say when it's time to stop one exercise and start the other.

Vocabulary words: exercise, healthy, pair, sideways, stretch, twins

Follow-up Ideas
Repeat this activity, but suggest children exercise from different positions, such as on their backs or sitting down. Incorporate objects such as streamers or paper plates into the exercises. Do the exercises to music. Use a signal to indicate when it's time to switch to the second exercise in the sequence (e.g., clap, ring a bell, change the music). Have children suggest a two-exercise sequence to use at transitions. Later in the year, depending on children's developmental and ability levels, try three- and four-sequence exercises.

Food Farm

What Children Do and Learn

Children move by pretending they are different types of food, taking turns as leaders and describing and demonstrating whole-body motions for others to follow.

Content area:
Physical Development and Health

Time of day:
Large-group time

Materials
For each child and teacher: None

To share: None

For backup: None

Story Starter

Down on the food farm, all the food got together for a day of fun and games. The first to arrive were the apples. Because they were all round, they rolled around the farm. Roll and encourage the children to roll too. *Next came spaghetti. The long, slippery strands slithered and slid along the ground.* Slide and wiggle on the ground and invite children to do the same. *Popcorn came too. How do you think it moved?* Solicit and act out children's ideas (e.g., jump up and down). *What other food is here, and how does it move?*

Scaffolding Children's Learning

Encourage children to name a food and describe and act out its movement for others to copy. Children may just move or name a food or action without demonstrating it. Build on their ideas. Ask how the food moves. If a child cannot think of a movement, ask others for suggestions. If a child does a movement, ask others to guess what food it could be. Offer challenges (e.g., *I'm a pancake. How should I move?*), or invite a child to be a peanut butter sandwich with you and walk with your hands stuck together. Children may also choose to add sound effects, such as *pop, pop* for popcorn or whistling for boiling tea.

Vocabulary words: *jump, roll, slippery, slide, slither, strand, wiggle*

Follow-up Ideas

When you cook food with children, describe and encourage them to act out the movements of the cooking process (e.g., how ingredients tangle together in the mixing bowl, swell or puff up with heat, or shrink as they lose moisture). When children pretend to cook in the house area, wonder aloud how the food they are cooking would move. Encourage children to describe how the food they eat at snacktimes and mealtimes moves on their plates (e.g., how the peas roll). Include foods that are familiar to children from those their families eat at home.

79 Going on a Hike

Content area:
Physical Development and Health

Time of day:
Large-group time

Materials
For each child and teacher: None

To share: Woodland "features" distributed throughout the room, such as hoops or tires as bodies of water; strips of butcher paper or fabric taped down as paths; railroad ties or long narrow blocks as logs; sturdy blocks piled pyramid-like as bridges; blankets draped over tables, chairs, or easels as caves; and so on

For backup: Additional blocks, rolls of fabric, and strips of paper for children to create other woodland features (e.g., rivers and streams, piles of leaves, mountains)

What Children Do and Learn
Children move in different ways over, under, around, and through various obstacles as they pretend to go on a hike in the woods.

Story Starter
Attention campers! It's time to hike through the woods. Walk to a strip of paper. *Let's start on this path. I can walk down the path straight* (walk straight) *or zigzag* (walk zigzag). *I wonder how you'll walk down the path.* Encourage children to walk on, alongside, or around the path in different ways. Go to a hoop. *Here we are at the lake. It's a hot day* (fan yourself with your hand), *so I'm going to jump in the lake to cool off.* Jump in the middle and out the other side. Encourage the children to choose their own way to move in or around the lake. Say *I wonder what else is here and how we'll move through the woods.*

Scaffolding Children's Learning
Describe, and encourage children to describe, how they move over, under, around, and through the woodland features. Pay attention to how they move their bodies as a whole, as well as to what they do with their arms and hands, legs and feet. Imitate and label their movements (e.g., *Sheldon is crawling into the cave on his elbows and knees. Marcy's feet are on either side of the log; she's straddling it*). Add and label other actions for children to imitate or extend in their own way (e.g., *I'm testing the water temperature with my toe before I decide if it's warm enough to go in*). Ask what part of the woods children are in. Repeat their words and add labels for less familiar features such as a rock overhang, valley, or creek.

Vocabulary words: balance, hike, straddling, straight, woods, zigzag

Follow-up Ideas

Provide equipment and materials for children to create their own woodlands, other natural landscapes they're familiar with (e.g., a beach and shoreline), manmade settings, or other obstacle courses. Encourage them to make props to support their play, such as tearing or cutting scraps of paper to represent a pile of leaves, or spreading a blanket for the ocean. Play the game outside, incorporating features of the natural landscape, such as puddles, hills, holes, tree stumps, fallen logs, boulders, and patches of dirt and grass. Look at pictures of woodlands or other settings of interest to the children, and have them recreate and act out how they would move through the various features. Take photos so children can recall and describe what they did.

This activity can be done outside, using features of the natural landscape. Children can pretend that props such as hoops or tires are bodies of water as they move through the outdoor environment.

80 Silent Sal

Content area:
Physical Development and Health

Time of day:
Large-group time

Materials
For each child and teacher: None

To share: None

For backup:
Scarves for children to wrap around their "sore throats"

What Children Do and Learn
Children act out a message for others to guess, using only body movements, gestures, and facial expressions.

Story Starter
Silent Sal had a sore throat. Put your hand on your throat with a sad expression. *It hurt to talk. So he moved his body or made a facial expression to show what he was thinking. If he wanted help getting his teddy bear down from the shelf, he pointed up* (point upwards) *and pretended to rock the bear* (cradle and rock your arms). *How do you suppose he showed he was sleepy and wanted to go to bed?* Solicit and act out the children's ideas. Rub your stomach and make eating motions, and ask *What do you think Sal was trying to say when he did this?* Solicit children's ideas. *Let's see if we can guess what you want to tell us without your talking.*

Scaffolding Children's Learning
Encourage each child who wants to take a turn acting out a simple message for others to guess. Remind them they can use facial expressions as well as movements and gestures. If a child acts out a message and also uses words to communicate (some may not yet grasp the idea of pantomime), accept what they say and do, and describe and copy the motions. If children get stumped, help by describing their actions and offering clues (e.g., *Kendra is moving her arm behind her head and pitching it forward. Do you suppose she's playing with a kind of toy?*). Make general suggestions (e.g., *Can you show us something you do at outside time for us to guess?*).

Vocabulary words: *body, facial expression, gesture, movement, silent*

Follow-up Ideas
At message board time, occasionally act out a message for children to guess. Use this strategy for planning or recall. Encourage children to act out something they will do (or did) at work (choice) time for you and the other children to guess. Children may want to develop a nonverbal signal for when others do or do not guess correctly, such as nodding yes or no. When children ask for help (provided they are not frustrated or impatient), suggest they act out their request for you to guess. If you miss after two tries, ask them to tell you.

Spotlight Hunt

81

What Children Do and Learn

Children guess which area of the room is lit by a flashlight, then follow movement directions to go to that spot.

Story Starter

The elves are sending us on a "spotlight hunt." Discuss what elves are (i.e., little "magic" people), and ask what the children think a spotlight hunt is. *A spotlight hunt has two clues. First, an elf shines a spotlight at a part of the room and we have to guess where it's shining.* Shine the flashlight at an area of the room (e.g., the easel in the art area), and encourage children to guess where the light is pointing. *After we guess where the light is shining, another elf gives us a clue about how to move there.* Pretend to listen to an elf (e.g., bend and cup your hand around your ear), and give a direction that lets children vary it in their own way (e.g., *The elf says we should move to the easel with our arms over our heads*). Move there with the children. Repeat the first two steps (e.g., shine the flashlight, ask children to guess the location), and say *The elf says to move to the bookshelf backwards*). Then continue by saying *I wonder where else the elves will shine the spotlight and how they will tell us to move there.*

Content area:
Physical Development and Health

Time of day:
Large-group time

Materials
For each child and teacher: None

To share: Flashlight

For backup: Extra flashlights

Children can take turns shining the flashlight on an area and saying how to move there. This activity can help children who are new to the program get acquainted with classroom areas and materials.

Scaffolding Children's Learning

Have children take turns shining the flashlight on an area and saying how to move there. One child may do both, or you can involve two children. Depending on children's familiarity with the areas and materials, they may name the area or a specific location within it (e.g., the large-group rug or the red square in the middle of the rug). If a child just shines the flashlight around the room, say something like *It looks like the elf is deciding where to shine the light. I wonder where it will stop.* As children carry out the movements, describe and encourage them to describe their actions (e.g., *Carl is turning his head to see where he's going as he walks backwards; Gina is switching which foot goes first while she slides to the water table*).

Vocabulary words: *backwards, clue, elf (elves), flashlight, hunt, shine, spotlight*

Follow-up Ideas

Use this activity at the beginning of the year to help acquaint children with the areas and materials in the room. After children are familiar with the game, add a third element by starting with a clue (e.g., *The elf is going to shine the spotlight on a part of the room where we paint*). Have the children guess the location, then shine the flashlight and ask if they did (not) guess right. Add extra flashlights to the classroom for children to use in their play. At planning time, have children point a flashlight at the area where they will play. At recall time, have them shine the flashlight at a material they used during work (choice) time.

Statue Land

82

Content area:
Physical
Development
and Health

Time of day:
Large-group time

Materials
For each child and teacher: None

To share: Bell

For backup:
Music player and
an instrumental
selection or simple
instrument (e.g.,
triangle) that can be
used to signal stop
and start movements

What Children Do and Learn
Children stop and start moving in response to a signal and describe the positions they freeze in.

Story Starter
The Wicked Witch put a spell on the people of Statue Land. Discuss what a statue is (i.e., a figure made of stone or wood that doesn't move). *Whenever the Wicked Witch rang a bell, the people had to stop what they were doing and freeze in place like statues until the witch rang the bell again. For example, if they were bending and she rang the bell, they froze in place like this* (demonstrate). *When the witch rang the bell, they could bend again* (demonstrate). *Let's all start to move. I'll be the witch* (gently laugh *heh-heh-heh*) *and when I ring the bell, freeze in place like statues.*

Scaffolding Children's Learning
Let children move for a while, then ring the bell. At first, you may need to also say *stop.* Comment on their poses using position and direction words (e.g., *Penny's leg is frozen in midair. Joshua's arm is high above his head*). Encourage them to describe their own and one another's positions. Ring the bell again for the children to resume moving. Again, the first few times, you may to also need to say *start.* Warn children that *Sometimes the witch waits a* long *time before she rings the bell again!* After a few rounds, have the children take turns as the witch (or they might prefer to be the good fairy) who rings the bell.

Vocabulary words: again, freeze, froze, in place, start, statue, stop

Follow-up Ideas
Repeat this activity, signaling stopping and starting with music from a CD, sounds from an instrument, and/or other signals (e.g., flicking lights off and on). Have one child move and freeze, then ask the others to describe and imitate that position. Play stop-and-start games at cleanup and transitions. When you join children's play, ask for stop-and-start cues (e.g., *How will I know when the cookie batter is ready and I can stop stirring it?*). Teach them the American Sign Language signs for stop (right hand chops down on open palm of left hand) and start (right index finger makes a "cranking" motion in the V formed by the left index and middle finger).

83 Up-in-the-Air People

Content area:
Physical Development and Health

Time of day:
Large-group time

Materials
For each child and teacher: None

To share: None

For backup: None

What Children Do and Learn
Children lie on their backs and move their legs and feet in the air, describing their motions and what they represent.

Story Starter
Once upon a time, in a faraway land, there were men and women and girls and boys called Up-in-the-Air People. *Why do you suppose they were called* Up-in-the-Air People? Solicit the children's ideas. *They got their name because they moved with their legs and feet up in the air instead of on the ground. This is how the grown-ups walked to work.* Lie on your back with your feet in the air and make walking motions with your legs. *And this is how the children ran to school when they were late.* Make running motions with your legs. Invite children to lie on their backs with their feet in the air. *How else do the Up-in-the-Air people move?*

As a follow-up activity, teachers can play a variety of musical selections as children lie on their backs and move their legs to the different tempos.

Scaffolding Children's Learning

Encourage children to describe and name their actions (e.g., *Eli is pumping his legs up and down. He says that's how Up-in-the-Air People climb stairs*). Give prompts (e.g., *I wonder how Up-in-the-Air People dance (ride their bicycles, skate, swim)? What do they do when it's time to eat? How do they put on their jackets?*). Imitate the children's movements. If they don't say what they're doing, ask *What do you call it when you move that way?* Ask children to name and describe your motions and guess what you're doing. Offer challenges (e.g., *I wonder how Up-in-the-Air People move only their feet but not their legs*).

Vocabulary words: *air, climb, cycle, ground, pump, skate, up*

Follow-up Ideas

Play music of varying tempos as children lie on their backs and move their legs to the music. Invite them to transition to different activities on their backs (e.g., scooting forward with their heels; propelling backwards with their elbows). At small-group time, use small figures with moveable legs to demonstrate different motions from a prone position. Provide art materials for children to represent objects and people engaged in different actions while lying on their backs. Do a "down-on-the-ground" small- or large-group activity where children move their arms, legs, and heads in different ways while lying on their stomachs.

84　Where's My Partner?

Content area:
Physical Development and Health

Time of day:
Small-group time

Materials
For each child and teacher: 6–8 pairs of nuts and bolts in different sizes; leave 2 sets assembled and disassemble the rest

To share: None

For backup: Pieces of plywood or cardboard with holes for children to fit nuts and bolts through

What Children Do and Learn
Children sort through separated nuts and bolts to find and reassemble matched pairs.

Story Starter
The nuts and bolts were cuddled together and snug in their beds. Hold up an assembled nut and bolt. *Suddenly, a big storm came along. Whoosh! The wind lifted the nuts and bolts out of their beds and separated them from their partners. They were scattered all over.* Separate a nut and bolt, setting each part down in a different place on the table. *The nuts and bolts were lonely and went looking for their partners.* Find and reassemble a pair. Give out the materials and say *Let's help more nuts and bolts get back together.*

Scaffolding Children's Learning
Encourage children to explore screwing and unscrewing the nuts and bolts. Describe, and encourage the children to describe, their motions. Comment on the size and fit of the pairs. Ask for the children's help (e.g., *I'm looking for a wider nut that this bolt will fit through. Can you help me find one?*). Talk with the children about where they've seen nuts and bolts used in construction projects at home or in the neighborhood (e.g., a shelving unit, a picnic table, or the scaffold of a building going up on the corner).

Vocabulary words: *bolt, nut, partner, scatter, screw (noun and verb), separated, twist, turn*

Follow-up Ideas
Put pieces of plywood and cardboard with holes, large-gauge mesh, and other materials with openings of different sizes in the block area for children to fit the nuts and bolts through. Add wrenches and other tools the children can use with nuts and bolts. Invite families to contribute hardware and tools they no longer use to the classroom. Use nuts and bolts in a math activity that focuses on counting (i.e., matching things in one-to-one correspondence). Provide containers for children to separate and sort the materials.

PART THREE: CREATING YOUR OWN STORY STARTERS

12

A Checklist for Creating Effective Story Starters

Though the activities you create for group times may start with a story, you should be well along in developing your ideas for the activity *before* you write the story. This may seem paradoxical, but it is important to remember that the story is a means to an end, not an end in itself. The purpose of using a story starter is to help children learn something — a skill, a set of information, or a concept — that has meaning to them and promotes their development. Unlike book reading, the story itself is not the focus of the interaction. However entertaining and engaging a story starter may be, it is merely the springboard to the activity that follows.

Suggested Sequence to Create Story Starter Activities

To create effective group activities that start with a story, it is helpful to follow these steps:

1. Decide on the content focus of the activity. Clarify the educational intention of the small- or large-group time. Identify the learning goals that are meaningful and appropriate for young children. The inspiration for the activity's focus can come from many sources, including the curriculum content areas and key developmental indicators, children's interests (e.g., what you observe in their spontaneous role-play or hear during their conversations at snacktime), an event such as a field trip or a visitor, or a new material you want to introduce to the classroom. List the skills, ideas, and types of problem solving you want children to explore, practice, and think about.

2. Identify relevant materials and actions. Review the first two ingredients of active learning — materials and manipulation (summarized below and described in chapter 4). Consider the variety of materials that engage children and support their learning in the content area you've chosen, for example, paired sets of objects that support one-to-one correspondence in counting, or three-dimensional art materials that elicit the use of multiple senses. Ask yourself the following questions: How might children use these materials alone and/or collaboratively? Are there particular actions that will help them learn basic skills or key concepts, such as putting together and taking apart objects or moving through and around obstacles in space? How can working with these materials and ideas spark young children's creative problem-solving and critical thinking skills?

3. Write the story. Now it's time to write a story that will arouse the children's curiosity and invite them to explore the materials, actions, and ideas you've identified in the previous steps. Build on the familiar and recurring topics in the children's play, such as pets, monsters, or going to the doctor. But also intrigue them with unusual subjects and perspectives, such as creatures who have strange physical features and quirky habits, or characters faced with absurd situations. Children enjoy humor, drama, and exaggeration. They also like language devices such as rhyme and alliteration. As you compose your narrative, follow the 10 principles for effective story starters (summarized below and detailed in chapter 3).

4. Plan scaffolding strategies. Anticipate the many ways children might respond to the story, use materials, and carry out their ideas. Think how to support and extend the learning of children at different developmental and ability levels. Be aware of when

you should acknowledge their current understanding (e.g., by imitating their actions and repeating their words) and when you can gently advance their thinking (e.g., by posing simple *What if...?* challenges). In sum, consider how to include in the activity the remaining three ingredients of active learning — choice, child language and thought, and adult scaffolding (summarized below and detailed in chapter 4).

5. Identify key vocabulary words. Part of scaffolding is enriching children's oral language. (See chapter 2 for a discussion of the importance of early language in later development). Look back over the story and scaffolding strategies, and choose a few key vocabulary words to introduce and use in conversations with the children. Don't expect them to understand and use these words themselves after just one activity. However, be alert to openings to use and repeat them in other group activities and parts of the daily routine throughout the year.

6. Generate follow-up ideas. Go back to your original content focus. How can you build on your story and scaffolding strategies to continue children's learning in this area? You can extend their experiences in two ways. First, consider the classroom and outdoor learning environment. Make sure children know the materials used in the activity are available at work (choice) time. Supplement them with related materials. Second, plan ways for children to engage with the ideas throughout the daily routine. Identify other small- or large-group activities that address the same content. Apply the materials and ideas at planning and recall time, message board, mealtimes, and transitions. Plan field trips and invite visitors to the classroom to extend children's exploration of related materials, imaginative role-play, and investigation of ideas. As you plan additional ways to follow up the activity, consider the role that families can play, including contributing materials, visiting the classroom to share their skills and interests, and carrying out related activities at home to support and extend their children's learning.

7. Revise your plan. The essence of good writing is revision. As you look back over your plan, change the story if it seems insufficiently related to the materials, too closed-ended or boring, or does not allow you to scaffold learning at different levels. Conversely, if the story seems rich with possibilities, anticipate additional ways it might inspire children, and add to your list of backup materials and scaffolding strategies accordingly.

8. Expect the unexpected. However much you plan, be open to where the story and the children's words and actions lead. Be flexible, and take your cues from what children say and do. Learn from the experience. If a story starter does not work the way you anticipated, identify its strengths and problems, modify it, and try it again.

Story Starter Checklist

You've organized your activity, listed the materials you'll need, and written your story starter. To maximize the success of your small- or large-group time, use the following checklist to fine-tune your plan as needed.

Content. What is the content of the activity?

- What content will the children learn?

- Why is this content important to learn?

- How can this content be made interesting to young children?

Active learning. Are the five ingredients of active learning present?

- *Materials:* Are the materials related to and appropriate for learning this content? Do you have enough materials for each child and adult? Are your backup materials readily available?

- *Manipulation:* How can children use these materials? Are they open-ended?

- *Choice:* Can children explore materials and ideas in different ways? Will children at all developmental and ability levels find something of interest in the activity?

- *Child language and thought:* Will children have opportunities to act, talk, and think about what they are doing and observing? Can they share their actions and ideas with adults and one another?

- *Adult scaffolding:* Are there strategies to differentiate and individualize learning for children at all developmental and ability levels? Will every child have a successful learning experience?

Story starter. Are the 10 characteristics of an effective story starter present? Review the list in chapter 3, then ask yourself the following 10 questions:

1. Is the story short?

2. Is the story simple?

3. Does the story follow a basic structure? Does it have a beginning, middle, and end? Are there interesting characters and events?

4. Have I practiced the story? Am I comfortable telling the story so I can focus on the children, not the recitation?

5. Where does the idea for the story originate? Have I considered why and how it will be of interest to the children?

6. Is the story open-ended? Does it invite children to contribute their own ideas?

7. Are there opportunities to introduce new vocabulary words to the children?

8. Is the story connected to the materials the children are using?

9. Am I narrating the story with the right amount of expression? Does my tone show I am interested in the characters and events? Am I turning my narration into a personal performance or can the children take ownership of the ideas and materials?

10. Does the story allow for children of different developmental and ability levels to engage with it?

Using the steps and checklist presented above, you are now ready to create your own story starter activities. The annotated activity plan in the following chapter will help you develop, and carry out story-based small- and large-group times with the young children in your program.

13

Your Ideas

This final chapter presents an annotated activity plan you can use to develop your own ideas for starting group activities with a story. It follows the same format as the story starters contained in this book, and contains a brief explanation and guidelines for completing each section.

Creating a Story Starter Activity Plan

Activity title: Although a title is optional, you may want to give your story and the associated activity a name. The name may be purely descriptive or you can have fun with it. A title is for your information rather than the children's, who do not need to know it in order to engage in the activity. For you, however, a title is a handy reference if you want to repeat, extend, or modify the story and activity at a later time. You may also experience a sense of satisfaction in creating a title, much as any creative writer uses one to communicate his or her ideas. Whether or not you assign a title, you may find that children invent their own descriptive names for activities, especially those that spark ideas for work (choice) time or other parts of the daily routine. For example, a child may say, *I'm hiding treasures like in the Captain Scrunch story.* A child's label is one indication that you've created a memorable story starter that "started" a child on the path of active learning.

Content area: Use this heading to specify the primary content focus of the small- or large-group activity. The content areas used in this book are from the HighScope Preschool Curriculum, namely[1]

- Language, Literacy, and Communication
- Mathematics
- Science and Technology
- Creative Arts: Art
- Creative Arts: Pretend Play
- Creative Arts: Music
- Physical Development and Health

You might choose to identify a more specific focus within a content area, for example, "alphabetic knowledge" within literacy, or "two-dimensional media" within art. If your program uses a curriculum other than High-Scope, use the names of the content areas of that curriculum. In sum, adapt this section to your program model, the children's interests, and the area(s) of learning you want the class to explore.

Time of day: Specify whether this activity is planned for small-group time or large-group time.

What Children Do and Learn

Building on the content area you've specified, write a short two-part statement. First, describe the kinds of activities — the actions, words, and problem-solving challenges — the children will engage in. Second, list the knowledge (i.e., facts, concepts) and skills they will gain in the process. Finally, if there are special considerations (e.g., the activity is best done outdoors or should follow a field trip to a location relevant to the story), you can also note that information. While the children will undoubtedly do and discover more than you capture in this brief statement, writing it will help you be thoughtful in planning the activity and intentional in the ways you scaffold their learning.

Materials

For each child and teacher:

List the materials that each child and teacher should have. Specify alternatives (including substitute materials) and quantities, and any other information that will help you be prepared.

To share:

List any materials that the group will share. Again, specify substitutes and quantities.

For backup:

List additional materials that should be available to support children's interests and allow them to take the activity in different directions.

Note that for some activities, such as a large-group movement or singing activity, there may not be any materials other than the children's own bodies or voices.

Story Starter

Write your story, using the 10 principles for effective story starters (see chapters 3 and 12). In addition to the narrative (that is, the story's words), include any directions to yourself regarding tone of voice, facial expressions or gestures, when to pause for the children's comments, when to distribute the materials, and so on.

---

[1]The content areas Social and Emotional Development and Social Studies are not used as the specific content focus for group-time activities. Rather, adults in HighScope settings take advantage of naturally occurring situations throughout the program day to help children learn and practice knowledge and skills in these areas.

Scaffolding Children's Learning

Briefly record your ideas for supporting and extending the learning of children at different developmental and ability levels. Make sure you have strategies in mind for those at earlier, middle, and later levels of development so every child can be involved and successful. Think about the cues — the actions and words — children present that will help you identify their level and the appropriate scaffolding techniques.

Vocabulary words: List a few relevant vocabulary words to introduce as you converse with the children. Remember that children need to hear words repeated and in context (not in isolation) before they understand and use the words themselves. Refer to this list after you complete an activity, and look for opportunities to use the words again in conversation as you build on the children's interests and extend their learning.

Follow-up Ideas

Think of ways to extend the learning throughout the room (i.e., the learning environment). Consider, for example, where to store the materials from the activity so children can continue to work with them, and add or reintroduce related materials to different areas of the classroom. Also, look for opportunities to extend children's learning throughout the program day (the daily routine). Relate elements of the activity to other small- and large-group times, words and images for the message board, planning and recall ideas, opportunities unique to outside time, transition times, and field trips.

Think of ways that families can contribute materials, share their interests and skills, and extend the activities at home. Plans for follow-up may also include repeating the activity, perhaps by varying the story and/or materials to further the children's learning. After completing the activity, be open to follow-up ideas that originate with the children themselves, during work (choice) time and other parts of the day.

A Final Story Starter for Readers of This Book

There was once a preschool teacher who had to come up with an activity for small-group time and for large-group time five days a week, every week. It was easy at first. There were so many materials to introduce, that at small-group time the teacher barely had to set them down before the children were eagerly exploring them. At large-group time, the teacher had only to begin moving or singing before the children wriggled and made up their own music. But after a while, the teacher wondered if there were other wells of ideas to dip into. That weekend, the teacher happened to read a book of short stories. Each story introduced new characters, vivid scenes, and surprising events. The teacher admired the author's endless imagination and realized, "I can use stories as another way to start group times too. After thousands of years, writers are still creating new stories all the time. I won't run out of ideas either." From then on, the teacher regularly used story starters as one of many strategies to begin small- and large-group times. The stories transported children to old and new places, connected them with ordinary and peculiar people, and presented them with familiar and unusual prob-

lems. I wonder what story starters you will create to share with and inspire the children in your program.

Stories take us places we've never been, introduce us to people we've never met, and involve us in experiences we've never had. Create story starters that will take you and the children on a journey of mutual discovery. Use your imagination to capture theirs. Start the adventure with a story, then let the children take it from there. You and they will never run out of ideas, revelations, and wellsprings of learning.

May the rope on your bucket go deeper than the water in your well.
— Old blessing (*Anonymous*)

Story Starters

References

Boisvert, C., & Gainsley, S. (2006). *50 large-group activities for active learners.* Ypsilanti, MI: HighScope Press.

Curenton, S. M. (2006, September). Research in review: Oral storytelling: A cultural art that promotes school readiness. *Young Children, 61*(5), 78–89.

Dickinson, D. K., & Tabors, P. O. (Eds.). (2001). *Beginning literacy with language: Young children learning at home and at school.* Baltimore: Paul H. Brookes.

Dickinson, D., & Tabors, P. O. (2002, March). Fostering language and literacy in classrooms and homes. *Young Children, 57*(2), 10–18.

Epstein, A. S. (2007a). *Essentials of active learning in preschool: Getting to know the HighScope Curriculum.* Ypsilanti, MI: HighScope Press.

Epstein, A. S. (2007b). *The intentional teacher: Choosing the best strategies for young children's learning.* Washington, DC: National Association for the Education of Young Children.

Epstein, A. S., Gainsley, S., Lockhart, S. D., Marshall, B., Neill, P., & Rush, K. (2009). *Small-group times to scaffold early learning.* Ypsilanti, MI: HighScope Press.

Flavell, J. H., & Miller, P. H. (1998). Social cognition. In D. Kuhn & R. S. Siegler (Eds.), *Cognition, perception, and language development: Handbook of child psychology* (5th ed., Vol. 2, pp. 851–898). New York: Wiley.

Gaffney, J. S., Ostrosky, M. M., & Hemmeter, M. L. (2008, July). Books as natural support for young children's literacy. *Young Children, 63*(4), 87–93.

Genishi, C., & Fassler, R. (1999). Oral language in the early childhood classroom: Building on diverse foundations. In C. Seefeldt (Ed.), *The early childhood curriculum: Current findings in theory and practice* (pp. 54–79). New York: Teachers College Press.

Goncu, A., & Klein, E. L. (2001). *Children in play, story, and school: A tribute to Greta Fein.* New York: Guilford Press.

Hart, B., & Risley, T. (1999). *The social world of children learning to talk.* Baltimore, MD: Paul H. Brookes.

Hohmann, M., & Adams, K. (2008). *Storybook talk: Conversations for comprehension.* Ypsilanti, MI: HighScope Press.

Hohmann, M., Weikart, D. P., & Epstein, A. S. (2008). *Educating young children: Active learning practices for preschool and child care programs* (3rd ed.). Ypsilanti, MI: HighScope Press.

Hurwitz, S. C. (2001, September). The teacher who would be Vivian. *Young Children, 56*(5), 89–91.

Isbell, R. T. (2002, March). Telling and retelling stories: Learning language and literacy. *Young Children, 57*(2), 26–30.

Jalongo, M. R. (2008). *Learning to listen, listening to learn: Building essential skills in young children.* Washington, DC: National Association for the Education of Young Children.

Kim, S. (1999). The effects of storytelling and pretend play on cognitive processes, short-term and long-term narrative recall. *Child Study Journal, 29*(3), 175–191.

Marshall, B., Lockhart, S. & Fewson, M. (2007). *HighScope step by step: Lesson plans for the first 30 days.* Ypsilanti, MI: HighScope Press.

McCabe, A. (1997). Developmental and cross-cultural aspects of children's narration. In M. Bamberg (Ed.), *Narrative development: Six approaches (pp. 137–174).* Mahwah, NJ: Erlbaum.

Moran, M. J., & Jarvis, J. (2001, September). Helping young children develop higher order thinking. *Young Children, 56*(5), 31–35.

National Reading Panel. (2000). *Teaching children to read: An evidence-based assessment of the scientific research literature on reading and its implication for reading instruction.* Washington, DC: National Institute for Child Health and Human Development, National Institutes of Health.

National Storytelling Network. (Undated). Retrieved from www.storynet.org.

Nelson, O. (1989). Storytelling: Language experience for meaning making. *The Reading Teacher, 42*(6), 386–390.

Nelson, K., & Fivush, R. (2004). The emergence of autobiographical memory: A sociocultural developmental theory. *Psychological Review, 111*(2), 486–511.

Neuman, S. B., Copple, C., & Bredekamp. S. (2000). *Learning to read and write: Developmentally appropriate practices for young children.* Washington, DC: National Association for the Education of Young Children.

Neuman, S. B., & Dickinson, D. K. (Eds.), (2001). *Handbook of early literacy research.* New York: Guilford Publications.

Paley, V. (1990). *The boy who would be a helicopter.* Cambridge, MA: Harvard University Press.

Ranweiler, L. W. (2004). *Preschool readers and writers: Early literacy strategies for teachers.* Ypsilanti, MI: HighScope Press.

Seuling, B. (2007, June). How to refine your picture book. *The Writer, 20*(6), 28–40.

Snow, C. E., Burns, M. S., & Griffin, P. (Eds.) (1998). *Preventing reading difficulties in young children: Committee on the Prevention of Reading Difficulties in Young Children, Commission on Behavioral and Social Sciences and Education, National Research Council.* Washington, DC: National Academy Press.

Storytelling ring. (10 July 2009) Retrieved from http://i.webring.com/hub?ring = storytelling

Trostle-Brand, S. L. & Donato, J. M. (2001). *Storytelling in emergent literacy: Fostering multiple intelligences.* Albany, NY: Delmar.

U. S. Department of Health and Human Services, Administration for Children and Families, Head Start Bureau. (2008, June 18). *Program Performance Standards and Other Regulations.* Retrieved from http://www.acf.hhs.gov/programs/ohs/legislation/index.html

Vygotsky, L. S. (1978). *Mind in society.* Cambridge, MA: Harvard University Press.

Whaley, C. (2002, March). Meeting the diverse needs of children through storytelling. *Young Children, 57*(2), 31–34.

Zimmerman, F. J., Gilkerson, J., Richards, J. A., Christakis, D. A., Xu, D., Gray, S., & Yapanel, U. (2009, July). Teaching by listening: The importance of adult-child conversations to language development. *Pediatrics, 124*(1), 342–349.

About the Author

Ann S. Epstein, PhD, is the Senior Director of Curriculum Development at the HighScope Educational Research Foundation in Ypsilanti, Michigan, where she has worked since 1975. She collaborates with a team of early childhood specialists to develop curriculum and staff training materials, develops program and child assessment tools, and evaluates federal, state, and local educational programs. Dr. Epstein has published numerous books and articles for professional and practitioner audiences, including *The Intentional Teacher, Essentials of Active Learning in Preschool: Getting to Know the HighScope Curriculum, Numbers Plus Preschool Mathematics Curriculum,* and *Me, You, Us: Social-Emotional Learning in Preschool,* and is co-author of *Educating Young Children, Supporting Young Artists,* and *Small-Group Times to Scaffold Early Learning.* Her short stories have appeared in *Emrys Journal, Clark Street Review, Passages North,* and *Red Rock Review.* She has a PhD in Developmental Psychology from the University of Michigan and also holds a Master's of Fine Arts degree from Eastern Michigan University.